Activities for
Teaching
Positive
Psychology

Activities for Teaching Positive Psychology

A Guide for Instructors

Edited by

Jeffrey J. Froh and Acacia C. Parks

American Psychological Association

Washington, DC

Second Printing, October 2013
Third Printing, February 2016

Published by
American Psychological Association
750 First Street, NE
Washington, DC 20002
www.apa.org

To order
APA Order Department
P.O. Box 92984
Washington, DC 20090-2984
Tel: (800) 374-2721; Direct: (202) 336-5510
Fax: (202) 336-5502; TDD/TTY: (202) 336-6123
Online: www.apa.org/pubs/books
E-mail: order@apa.org

In the U.K., Europe, Africa, and the Middle East, copies may be ordered from
American Psychological Association
3 Henrietta Street
Covent Garden, London
WC2E 8LU England

Typeset in Trump Medieval by Circle Graphics, Inc., Columbia, MD

Printer: Edwards Brothers, Inc., Ann Arbor, MI
Cover Designer: Minker Design, Bethesda, MD

The opinions and statements published are the responsibility of the authors, and such opinions and statements do not necessarily represent the policies of the American Psychological Association.

Library of Congress Cataloging-in-Publication Data

Activities for teaching positive psychology : a guide for instructors / edited by Jeffrey J. Froh and Acacia C. Parks. — 1st ed.
    p. cm.
  Includes bibliographical references and index.
  ISBN 978-1-4338-1236-1 — ISBN 1-4338-1236-3   1. Positive psychology—Study and teaching.
2. Positive psychology—Problems, exercises, etc. I. Froh, Jeffrey J. II. Parks, Acacia C.

  BF204.6.A26 2013
  150.19′88071—dc23
                                2012023266

British Library Cataloguing-in-Publication Data
A CIP record is available from the British Library.

Printed in the United States of America
First Edition

DOI: 10.1037/14042-000

To the three people who bring love, peace, and meaning to my life: Cara, James, and Julianne. And to Professor William Thieben, for showing me that to teach is to touch a soul.

—*Jeffrey J. Froh*

To my mother, my wishing star. Through your example, I have learned to carve my own way, and to do it with abandon, no matter where life may lead me.

—*Acacia C. Parks*

CONTENTS

CONTRIBUTORS

Lara B. Aknin, PhD, Assistant Professor, Simon Fraser University, Vancouver, British Columbia

Brett Anderson, MA, Northern Illinois University, DeKalb

Fred B. Bryant, PhD, Professor, Loyola University Chicago, Chicago, IL

Brian D. Christens, PhD, Assistant Professor, University of Wisconsin, Madison

William Damon, PhD, Professor, Director of the Stanford Center on Adolescence, Stanford University, Stanford, CA

Don E. Davis, PhD, Assistant Professor, Georgia State University, Atlanta

Elizabeth W. Dunn, PhD, Associate Professor, University of British Columbia, Vancouver

Robert A. Emmons, PhD, Professor, University of California, Davis

Yuna L. Ferguson, PhD, Assistant Professor, Penn State Shenango, Sharon, PA

Constance Flanagan, PhD, Professor, University of Wisconsin, Madison

Barbara L. Fredrickson, PhD, Professor, University of North Carolina at Chapel Hill

Jeffrey J. Froh, PsyD, Associate Professor, Hofstra University, Hempstead, NY

Shelly L. Gable, PhD, Professor, University of California, Santa Barbara

Aubrey L. Gartner, PhD, Postdoctoral Fellow, Veterans Affairs Medical Center, Durham, NC

Maria R. Gear Haugen, PhD, MBA, Clinical Psychologist, Lexington, KY

Patrick R. Harrison, MA, graduate student, Loyola University Chicago, Chicago, IL

Sara D. Hodges, PhD, Associate Professor, University of Oregon, Eugene

David J. Jennings II, MS, MA, doctoral student, Virginia Commonwealth University, Richmond

Todd B. Kashdan, PhD, Associate Professor of Psychology and Senior Scientist at the Center for Consciousness and Transformation, George Mason University, Fairfax, VA

Tim Kasser, PhD, Professor, Chair of Psychology, Knox College, Galesburg, IL

Bethany E. Kok, MA, doctoral candidate, University of North Carolina at Chapel Hill

Tara L. Kraft, MA, graduate student, University of Kansas, Lawrence

Jaime L. Kurtz, PhD, Assistant Professor, James Madison University, Harrisonburg, VA

Michelle C. Louis, PhD, Adjunct Assistant Professor, Bethel University, St. Paul, MN

Sonja Lyubomirsky, PhD, Professor, University of California, Riverside

Jeana L. Magyar-Moe, PhD, Associate Professor, University of Wisconsin–Stevens Point

Timothy R. Mariels, MA, graduate student, Santa Clara University, Santa Clara, CA

Christopher Michaelson, PhD, Associate Professor, University of St. Thomas Opus College of Business, Minneapolis–St. Paul, MN

Michael W. Myers, PhD, Visiting Assistant Professor, Showa University, Tokyo, Japan

Kenneth I. Pargament, PhD, Professor, Bowling Green State University, Bowling Green, OH

Acacia C. Parks, PhD, Assistant Professor, Hiram College, Hiram, OH

Jennifer Teramoto Pedrotti, PhD, Associate Professor, California Polytechnic State University, San Luis Obispo

Sarah D. Pressman, PhD, Assistant Professor, University of Kansas, Lawrence

Cynthia L. S. Pury, PhD, Professor, Clemson University, Clemson, SC
Timothy S. Reilly, BS, doctoral candidate, Stanford University, Stanford, CA
Christie Napa Scollon, PhD, Associate Professor, Singapore Management University
Shauna L. Shapiro, PhD, Associate Professor, Santa Clara University, Santa Clara, CA
Kennon M. Sheldon, PhD, Professor, University of Missouri, Columbia
David J. Shernoff, PhD, Associate Professor, Northern Illinois University, DeKalb
Paul J. Silvia, PhD, Associate Professor, University of North Carolina at Greensboro
Jennifer L. Smith, MA, doctoral candidate, Loyola University Chicago, Chicago, IL
Amy Sparrow, BA, master's student, Eastern Washington University, Cheney
Alan S. Waterman, PhD, Professor Emeritus, The College of New Jersey, Ewing
Philip C. Watkins, PhD, Professor, Eastern Washington University, Cheney
Amy C. Webber, BA, master's student, Eastern Washington University, Cheney
Derrick Wirtz, PhD, Associate Professor, East Carolina University, Greenville, NC
Xuan-yi Wei, BSocSc, Student, Singapore Management University
Everett L. Worthington Jr., PhD, Professor of Psychology, Virginia Commonwealth University, Richmond

PREFACE

Our book began from a simple observation: No two positive psychology textbooks cover the same set of topics, and as a result, no two positive psychology syllabi are the same. Although this may at first seem obvious—instructors and textbook writers put their personal stamps on the courses they teach and the books they write—the huge variation among positive psychology courses and textbooks is, in fact, an oddity compared with other, more established subareas of psychology. The few existing textbooks in positive psychology, although of high quality in their coverage of various topics, differ as much as they are similar in terms of which topics are included.

Fields like social, abnormal, and developmental psychology are, aside from small variations, somewhat homogenous, particularly when it comes to content covered. There are many good reasons for this. Uniformity in the content of a course makes it easier for new instructors to begin teaching that course, for an instructor to take over an existing course from someone else, for students to earn transfer credit and to pass standardized tests like the Psychology Graduate Record Exam or Advanced Placement exam, and for textbook writers to create appropriate teaching resources. However, positive psychology is a relatively new field, and furthermore, it is rapidly growing and expanding—there is no consensus about what topics belong under the umbrella of "positive psychology." Because of this lack of consensus, we have observed, anecdotally, a significant demand (on the Friends of Positive Psychology Listserv, for example) for guidance when it comes to designing a new positive psychology course. At present, no existing book answers the question, "What are my options in the teaching of positive psychology?" We decided that the solution to this problem is not another textbook, but a book that is designed for instructors. Furthermore, we thought, there is no teaching-oriented book in positive psychology wherein experts on each individual topic area provide advice on how to teach that topic. So, in the beginning, we knew two things about the book we wanted to create: Our target audience was instructors, and we wanted it to be an edited volume.

The next question we had to answer was, "What resources do positive psychology instructors need the most?" The answer, we quickly determined, was first and foremost a broad-sweeping overview of the field that encompasses all of the topics that are included in existing textbooks. Furthermore, based on reams of anecdotal evidence from instructors of positive psychology, it was clear to us that one of the most distinctive features of positive psychology as a course is its heavy reliance on hands-on experience with the concepts being taught. Again and again, students in our classes and the classes of our colleagues have praised the value of activities, both inside and outside the classroom, that help students put what they are learning into practice. The convergence of the above ideas resulted in the idea for this book: an edited volume containing hands-on activities designed by leading researchers and skilled teachers, each of which is intended to illustrate one of the seminal concepts in positive psychology and is accompanied by a succinct summary of each concept with references and suggested readings. This format is consistent with our desire to play to the strengths of positive psychology—emphasizing the hands-on experience that makes positive psychology courses so powerful—while also fulfilling our initial goal of providing a resource for instructors that spans the many topics that are encompassed by this new and dynamic field.

Both of us have taught positive psychology (we have 12 years of experience between us), and our courses have received positive reviews from students. As editors, we drew on these experiences to help our contributors build and refine activities that we were confident would be successful in the classroom. We were pleased to have had such a superstar cast of authors, who often dazzled us with not only their expertise but also their creativity in applying that expertise toward the purpose of teaching. The result of our efforts has far exceeded our expectations, and we are pleased to present to you what we hope will be a useful resource.

Making this book was a team effort. We first want to thank our acquisitions editor, Linda McCarter, for her guidance, expertise, and patience. This was our first edited book, and Linda made the process not only painless but fun. We thank her for giving us a shot and for believing in our idea and ability to edit this book. We are also grateful to Robert Biswas-Diener, Andrew Greene, and Charles Levinthal for their helpful comments on our original proposal and to Shane Lopez and Bob Emmons for their mentorship on navigating this process. We are thankful to Tyler Aune (and to his reviewers) for feedback and assistance during the final stretch of this project, as we got the manuscript ready for publication. Last, we are deeply grateful to all of our contributing authors. It is because of your willingness to help and dedication to teaching students about positive psychology and how to flourish that this book exists. In particular, we are grateful to those contributors whom we approached early on and who agreed to have their names included in the book proposal before we had even found a publisher. Your faith is humbling, and the warm reception our proposal received from the American Psychological Association was no doubt due in large part to the all-star lineup we brought to the table. We are fortunate to work with people who not only teach and study positive psychology but also *live* it.

Activities for Teaching Positive Psychology

INTRODUCTION
Jeffrey J. Froh and Acacia C. Parks

Positive psychology has bloomed into a burgeoning and ever-changing field that is of great interest to students. When offered at Harvard University in 2006, positive psychology was the single most popular course that year—and the most popular course in Harvard's history!—with more than 800 students enrolled. At the University of Pennsylvania, courses in positive psychology at all levels (introductory, seminar, and writing seminars) are regularly filled to their limit, with large waiting lists. Now, more than a decade since its inception, positive psychology is offered at myriad academic institutions at the high school, college, and graduate levels, and in numbers that continue to grow year after year.

Despite positive psychology's popularity as a subject, there are huge differences between one positive psychology course and the next. Unlike more established areas, such as abnormal and social psychology, a definitive, exhaustive positive psychology textbook has yet to be written; as a new and evolving field, a consensus as to which topics fall under the umbrella of positive psychology has not developed. Topics that are central in one textbook are not even mentioned in others. Some topics, such as mindfulness and self-determination theory, are relevant to the science of happiness and are often mentioned in positive psychology textbooks, but do not belong exclusively to positive psychology. Because they are also clearly central to certain psychological disorders and therapeutic orientations, they are also a part of clinical psychology and other related areas (e.g., personality psychology). Others, like empathy, are clearly relevant to positive psychology, yet they are featured in positive psychology courses only rarely in comparison with staples such as gratitude, meaning, and flow. Without any comprehensive resource to tell instructors what positive psychology *is*, designing a positive psychology course can involve a lot of legwork.

DOI: 10.1037/14042-001
Activities for Teaching Positive Psychology: A Guide for Instructors, J. J. Froh and A. C. Parks (Editors)

One of the overarching goals of this book, then, is to be that comprehensive resource. We aim to help instructors see the lay of the land, as it were, when it comes to positive psychology course design. It is a teaching activities book, but it is also, as the title says, a *guide* for instructors. We hope to accomplish more than simply tacking some activities on to your existing courses. In the remainder of this introduction, we outline the contents of this volume, but more than that, we tell you *how to use it.*

WHAT RESOURCES CAN I FIND IN THIS BOOK?

The 25 chapters herein are intended to facilitate learning via innovative activities created by the leading scholars and teachers in positive psychology. Each chapter contains the following sections:

- a *mini-abstract* that describes the activity in several sentences;
- a *Concept*, which briefly summarizes the relevant concepts and method of the activity and typically includes some in-text citations to direct the reader to more information about the relevant concepts;
- *Materials Needed*, which often include items contained in the appendices, as well as anything from pencils and paper to calculators and overhead projectors;
- *Instructions*, which describe how to execute the activity and include references to accompany the mention and definition of essential concepts (brief literature reviews are often found here, in the Discussion, or in both places depending on the flow of the chapter);
- a *Discussion*, which is a debriefing on the activity, including troubleshooting, ideas for class discussion after the activity is finished, and any other important information the instructor needs to make the activity effective for the students to learn;
- a *Writing Component* (optional), which helps students reflect on, synthesize, and integrate what they have learned;
- *References*, which include both in-text citations and suggested readings to help instructors and students better grasp the material; and
- *Resources*, such as worksheets, questionnaires, and interview questions needed to complete the activities in the book.

HOW CAN I USE THIS BOOK TO MEET MY NEEDS?

Positive psychology can be taught using popular texts, primary sources, or a textbook; via lecture or discussion; in person or online; to high school, undergraduate, and graduate students; and as an introductory level survey or advanced seminar (Parks, 2011). Regardless of the reader's commitment to a particular set of readings, preference for a group of topics to offer, desired audience, or style of teaching, this volume is designed to serve as a useful resource for any instructor in the psychology teaching community. To maximize utility for readers, we have identified three "types" of instructors who are likely to use this book and have taken pains to provide guidelines for each of these audiences in the structuring of our chapters.

There are several ways in which this book can be helpful for people who have never taught positive psychology before. First, simply leafing through the table of contents provides an overview of the field and of the many topics it comprises; this can be helpful in the initial stages of course planning. Although it would be wonderful to include all of the topics in this book in every positive psychology class we teach—we do believe that each topic uniquely contributes to understanding well-being—making tough choices is an inevitable part of course design, and depth is often more important than breadth when the goal is learning. This book aims to help new instructors explore their options and choose which topics they value most or find to be the most interesting.

Readers who have never taught positive psychology before should first familiarize themselves with the topics in the table of contents and then begin to create their ideal course. Each chapter provides an overview of relevant concepts so readers can get a sense of the range of topics available by reading the opening section ("Concept"). After the decision as to which topics to cover has been made, the papers cited in the References can aid in learning the topic and preparing lessons. Papers in the References section of each chapter can also be used as assigned readings for students. Some instructors will opt instead to use a textbook (see Rich, 2011, for an up-to-date comparison of textbook options) and nonscientific sources (see Jayawickreme & Forgeard, 2011, for some suggestions).

Although some readers may be planning to prepare a course entirely dedicated to positive psychology straightaway—many models for such courses certainly exist[1]—others may still be trying to figure out how and when to bring positive psychology content into a curriculum. As mentioned previously, the range of topics included under the umbrella of positive psychology is vast, and positive psychology content need not be restricted to courses called *positive psychology*. Thus, instructors may pick and choose topics based not only on interest but also on the fit between the topic and the course in which it will be featured.

Positive psychology can easily be added as a module in a general psychology course; the editors of this volume have done this on several occasions. Furthermore, models exist for bringing positive psychology content into existing courses in other subareas of psychology, including abnormal (Magyar-Moe, 2011), developmental (Marks, 2011), and judgment/decision making (Kurtz, 2011); however, the topics that are appropriate for inclusion in one course may be inappropriate for another course. For example, one of the editors (Parks) recently taught a course on personality and featured several relevant positive psychology topics, including positive emotions, motivation, character strengths, and empathy. In a clinical/counseling psychology elective she is currently designing, she is focusing on constructs such as gratitude, purpose, and forgiveness, which have been successfully changed via interventions.

---

[1]Both editors have made their syllabi available online (http://hiram.academia.edu/AcaciaParks and http://people.hofstra.edu/jeffrey_j_froh/Teaching.html). The University of Pennsylvania's Positive Psychology Center also has several syllabi posted on its website.

In summary, the new positive psychology instructor can use this book to gain a basic understanding of topics included under the umbrella of positive psychology and to assess where positive psychology might fit best in his or her department's curriculum: as a new course, as a new module of a course, or as a sprinkling of new content that is integrated into an existing psychology content area.

The Experienced Positive Psychology Instructor

Some readers will have taught positive psychology previously, perhaps with an existing textbook, but may want to go into greater depth on certain concepts. Readers who fit in this category have taught positive psychology several times and as a result have a solid understanding of the literature coupled with an arsenal of high-quality lectures and discussions. Experienced instructors have probably also asked students to gain hands-on experience with research-based happiness techniques by going on a "gratitude visit" or "thinking about their best possible selves" between class sessions. Activities such as these, which are derived from seminal positive psychology studies, can be limiting because they are relevant only for a handful of topics (gratitude, strengths, savoring, and hope). Thus, one aim of this book is to go beyond the handful of exercises that can already be found in the positive psychology literature (see Parks & Biswas-Diener, in press, for a comprehensive review), presenting activities on topics for which no activities have previously been proposed. These activities allow instructors to be more comprehensive in their use of experiential learning rather than being limited to the handful of topics for which empirically supported interventions exist.

Experienced teachers of positive psychology may also wonder how they might raise student engagement during the class period itself, aside from the more traditional lecture and discussion formats. Although we certainly believe that hands-on out-of-class experiences are an essential component of teaching of positive psychology, we also believe in the value of in-class activities and demonstrations, and we sought to provide more of those types of activities in this volume. As mentioned previously, most existing positive psychology activities are intervention focused. By definition, happiness-increasing techniques are generally practiced in students' day-to-day lives, where the instructor cannot guarantee that the experience will be instructive—or that it will take place at all for that matter! We also sought, in this volume, to provide alternatives to the out-of-class interventions often used to demonstrate topics like gratitude and strengths. Such activities allow instructors to keep the topics already covered in their courses but cover them in more depth by including in-class structured activities.

In summary, one of our motivations for creating this book was to address what we saw as a lack of variety in available activities and a lack of nonintervention activities that could be performed in class. Experienced instructors can use the activities herein to flesh out their treatment of topics that they are already covering or to supplement the out-of-class activities.

The Expert Positive Psychology Instructor

Seasoned instructors who are familiar with the content areas of positive psychology may be looking to branch out into new topic areas or to teach positive psychology in less traditional settings. For example, positive psychology can serve as an excellent backdrop for training students in research methods (Kim-Prieto & D'Oriano, 2011), as one of the editors (Froh) has done; the other editor (Parks) has used positive psychology course content as the foundation of a freshman critical writing course (Parks & Ross, in press). In both of these situations, the instructor is faced with conveying relatively dry content ("nuts and bolts" as it were), and he or she has the opportunity, with activities like those featured in this book, to bring that content to life. We have observed that hands-on experiences with happiness and happiness-related concepts provide an excellent source of ideas for both research projects (in the case of a research methods course) and essay topics (in the case of a writing course). Personal investment in a topic engenders an enthusiasm that reading and discussing from a distance often fail to.

As an expert on positive psychology, the advanced instructor may also be asked to give guest lectures in courses outside of psychology, including education and business. For example, one of the editors (Parks) gave a guest presentation on strengths in an organizational development course at the Wharton School of Business. She spoke for an hour and a half on strengths and then conducted a brief group activity in which students were asked to consider their own strengths.[2] Several months later, she spoke to a student who had attended that lecture. The student remembered one thing above all else: what he had learned, through the in-class activity, about how to use his own strengths at work. In such circumstances, where the instructor aims to leave a lasting impression, a half hour of a well-done in-class activity can have more of an impact than an hour spent lecturing.

Finally, with recent trends toward interdisciplinary programs, experts in positive psychology may be asked to coteach a course with a faculty member in another discipline. One of the editors (Parks) is developing a health psychology course, which will be cotaught with a professor in biomedical humanities. The collaborator studies people's personal narratives surrounding health, and so the positive psychology content in this course will come largely from topics such as positive health, spirituality and purpose (around issues of death and dying), motivation (to pursue health behaviors), and gratitude (an emotion with clearly demonstrated links to physical health). Depending on the collaboration, different positive psychology topics will be more or less relevant to different interdisciplinary courses.

WHAT KINDS OF ACTIVITIES ARE IN THIS BOOK, AND WHEN IS IT APPROPRIATE TO USE THEM?

The activities in this book are classified into three groups, each of which is appropriate for use at different times in a class. The activities in the first group, the *conceptual explorations*, provide structured ways to immerse students in the most essential concepts related to a topic. One way to use these activities is as an introduction to a topic before lecture (in a larger survey course) or more in-depth discussion (in a seminar course). They can also provide a way of making abstract concepts introduced in lecture more concrete. For example, the chapter on strengths (Chapter 2) asks students to consider ways in which different personal strengths could contribute to success in

---

[2]She notes that Michelle Louis's strengths activity in this volume would have been a perfect addition, had it only existed at that time!

dealing with a particular life challenge, such as resolving an interpersonal conflict. This activity could be used as a prelude to a more technical discussion of strengths, giving students a sense of personal involvement in the topic. Alternatively, it could serve to crystallize what students have learned about strengths by considering ways that strengths can be practically applied. Each activity in this section can play either of these roles, depending on instructor preference.

The second group of activities, the *experiments*, is intended to demonstrate concepts in class by making students "participants" in a simulated experiment. For example, the empathy activity (Chapter 12) involves giving students one of two vignettes. The first is designed to induce empathy and the second to undermine empathy. Students then complete an empathy survey, and the two groups compare their results. Like conceptual explorations, experiments can be used on naïve students or on students who have already read about and discussed a topic extensively. Demonstrations can provide a vivid illustration of a concept to students who have not yet been exposed to it, which helps to stimulate interest in subsequent lectures and discussions. Actually experiencing, in the moment, the phenomenon they are learning about can be a powerful experience. Students who have background in the topic benefit in a different way. Prior knowledge of existing research—in the case of empathy, for example, the induction used in class is often used in research studies to induce empathy—allows students to observe the demonstration analytically and encourages them to think critically about the experimental methods that are used to study that topic.

Personal experience/self-reflections take what has been learned in class and bring it into real-world practice. Some of these activities take place in class and others out of class, but all activities in this category have in common the requirement that students tie concepts to themselves and to their own lives. While these activities *can* be used to introduce topics, they are, in our opinion, best used as a way to conclude discussion on a topic. When students have had the chance to learn about a topic academically and to experience it personally, some exciting discussions can—and often do—ensue in class.

SUMMARY

You have now learned that our book is a resource for new, experienced, or expert instructors teaching positive psychology at the high school, undergraduate, and graduate levels. Offering a buffet of positive psychology topics with an in-depth class activity for each, this book will help you familiarize yourself with the ever-expanding field of positive psychology. The suggested activities use varied methods but have in common the fact that they originate from leading thinkers and teachers in the field of positive psychology. These activities are the ideal complement to any positive psychology course, be it one that revolves around a textbook or around primary source readings. By increasing student engagement through these hands-on activities, you will in turn observe an increase in your own engagement as an instructor; it is this genuine passion for the field that will place *your* course among the ranks of positive psychology courses that students praise as "life changing."

REFERENCES

Jayawickreme, E., & Forgeard, M. J. C. (2011). Insight or data: Using non-scientific sources to teach positive psychology. *The Journal of Positive Psychology, 6,* 499–505. doi:10.1080/17439760.2011.634819

Kim-Prieto, C., & D'Oriano, C. (2011). Integrating research training and the teaching of positive psychology. *The Journal of Positive Psychology, 6,* 457–462. doi:10.1080/17439760.2011.634827

Kurtz, J. L. (2011). Happiness and self-knowledge: A positive psychology and judgment and decision-making hybrid course. *The Journal of Positive Psychology, 6,* 463–467. doi:10.1080/17439760.2011.634820

Magyar-Moe, J. L. (2011). Incorporating positive psychology content and applications into various psychology courses. *The Journal of Positive Psychology, 6,* 451–456. doi:10.1080/17439760.2011.634821

Marks, P. E. L. (2011). Adolescent popularity: A positive psychology course with a developmental foundation. *The Journal of Positive Psychology, 6,* 314–319. doi:10.1080/17439760.2011.580772

Parks, A. C. (2011). The state of positive psychology in higher education: Introduction to the special issue. *The Journal of Positive Psychology, 6,* 429–431. doi:10.1080/17439760.2011.637729

Parks, A. C., & Biswas-Diener, R. (in press). Positive interventions: Past, present and future. In T. Kashdan, & J. Ciarrochi, (Eds.), *Bridging acceptance and commitment therapy and positive psychology: A practitioner's guide to a unifying framework.* Oakland, CA: New Harbinger.

Parks, A. C., & Ross, V. (in press). Writing critically about personal growth: A "writing in the disciplines" course on happiness. In A. C. Parks, (Ed.), *Positive psychology in higher education.* London, England: Taylor & Francis.

Rich, G. (2011). Teaching tools for positive psychology: A comparison of available textbooks. *The Journal of Positive Psychology, 6,* 492–498. doi:10.1080/17439760.2011.634824

I
CONCEPTUAL
EXPLORATIONS

PURPOSE

In the activities in this part of the book, the class examines the nature of a concept and its relevant processes through discussion and writing. Students are called on to put abstract concepts to use, considering how these concepts matter to us and how they come into play in everyday life.

OVERVIEW OF ACTIVITIES

Cynthia L. S. Pury offers a structured discussion activity on **Courage**, which allows students to define the essential features of courage, distinguish between different types of courage, and understand the processes by which courage can occur. Robert A. Emmons illustrates the concept of **Humility** with an activity in which students describe individuals they consider to be exemplars of humility, then use those exemplars to draw broad conclusions about what does and does not make a person humble. Michelle C. Louis asks students to explore the meaning of various **Strengths** by brainstorming ways in which a given strength can be used to approach a particular problem or challenge. Alan S. Waterman's structured discussion revolves around the difference between more traditional pleasure-focused conceptions of "happiness" and **Eudaimonia**; after completing a questionnaire that measures hedonia and eudaimonia, students generate scores for each form of happiness and then compare and contrast them and discuss their role in achieving one's best potentials. Christopher Michaelson helps students explore the importance of **Work** in determining an individual's well-being; after generating a list of types of work and plotting them on a matrix, students discuss the role of work in living the good life. Jennifer Teramoto Pedrotti encourages students to consider the relationship between **Culture and Identity**, asking students to consider which aspects of their cultural background may have led to the development of their most salient and valued positive personality. Timothy S. Reilly and William Damon have students interview each other as a way of understanding what factors converge to determine an individual's sense of **Purpose**. In Maria R. Gear Haugen and Kenneth Pargament's activity, students interview a person who has experienced adversity and ask the interviewee to consider the role that **Spirituality** may or may not have played in their thoughts, feelings, and behaviors.

1

COURAGE
WHAT MAKES AN ACTION COURAGEOUS?
Cynthia L. S. Pury

This flexible in-class exercise can be used to illustrate and lead into class discussions about multiple features of courage, including types of courageous behavior, defining features of courage, the role of fear in courage, the difference between courage as an accolade and courage as a process, and the role of success in accolade courage.

CONCEPT

This exercise hinges on a basic retrospective narrative: Describe a time you acted courageously. Variations in the narrative instruction can be given to highlight different areas of courage research.

MATERIALS NEEDED

Separate sheets of paper for each student, pen/pencil for each student, whiteboard, and whiteboard markers.

INSTRUCTIONS

Because this activity is designed to introduce the concept of courage and explore its various forms and definitions, it is best placed at the beginning of a class discussion on courage. Before reading the exercise to students, select the variation(s) you will use, and be sure to read the additional instructions.

Instructions: Students will write for about 5 minutes on a variation of a basic prompt, then trade responses and discuss the response that they have received. Before beginning, read the following warning: *Your answers to this exercise will be traded with another student who may read it out loud to the class: Make sure you write about something you feel comfortable sharing. Do not put your name on the paper.*

Main Prompt: Describe a time you acted courageously. Why was it courageous? What were you thinking and feeling? Describe what led up to your action, the action itself, and the outcome of your action. Many of the variations listed below have additional prompts that will be inserted at the end of this basic one. In all cases, students should write just one narrative, with additional prompts as needed.

After students finish writing, ask them to fold their papers in half with the writing inside, stand up, and trade papers with someone on the opposite side of the room. Then ask them to trade again. This allows students to feel some distance from the acts they will be discussing and limits potential modesty (false or otherwise) that students may feel in describing what they did.

DOI: 10.1037/14042-002
Activities for Teaching Positive Psychology: A Guide for Instructors, J. J. Froh and A. C. Parks (Editors)

Types of Courageous Acts: This activity requires no additional prompt; the basic prompt typically generates a range of responses, including acts that illustrate each of the three main types of courage. A summary of typical responses for college students can be found in Pury, Kowalski, and Spearman (2007). The most commonly reported physically courageous actions were preventing injury due to a dangerous environment and helping an injured person. The most commonly reported psychologically courageous actions were stepping outside of one's comfort zone to try something new and helping out in a medical crisis that was *not* caused by an accident. Finally, the most commonly reported morally courageous acts were standing up to others for what is right and taking responsibility for a negative situation (Pury et al., 2007).[1]

After the written courage stories have been traded, tell students about the three main types of courageous actions (physical, moral, psychological) described above. Ask them to think about what type(s) best describe the action they have in their hands and why, then create four columns on the whiteboard with the labels "Physical," "Moral," "Psychological," and "Other." Ask students to read the action they are holding and tell you which column it belongs in and why and then write a short summary of the action in the column selected by the student (or reclassified by you or the class if different).

As an alternative, if more class time is available, instructors can ask students to identify what they think are the common types based on class data rather than tell students about different types of courage. These class-generated types can then be used as a springboard for discussion of the types of courage typically described by researchers, with differences and similarities highlighted.

Defining Features: After students trade stories, describe the basic features of courageous actions described in Rate (2010). Create three columns on the board ("Willing/ Intentional," "Noble/Worthy Goal," and "Risk or Difficulty"). Ask students to read the narrative they have been handed to themselves, then mark any areas that describe intentionality, worthiness of goal, or risk or difficulty. In my experience, these features are commonly found both in the story and in the reasons why the action was courageous. Ask for a show of hands of students who found each of the three main features, and record the results on the board. Ask for examples of each of the features and discuss.

Role of Success in Accolade Courage: After students have finished writing and switched stories, ask them to read the narrative they have been handed, to mark or write down the goal the person was trying to accomplish, and whether the person accomplished that goal. Write "Yes" and "No" on the board. Go around the room, asking students for the goal of the action they are holding and whether it was accomplished. Discuss in the context of Pury and Hensel (2010) described below.

Ethics and Courage Research: After writing on the prompt(s) selected and discussion, you can end this section by describing the retrospective narrative method employed in current courage research. What do students see as the advantages and disadvantages of such methods? Why are more true experiments not designed to test

---

[1]Instructors might worry that students will not give responses indicative of less prototypical types of courage: that is, instances of moral or psychological courage. I believe this is unlikely: We have asked this basic question to hundreds of undergraduates without preamble in various research studies. In each case, it generates the range of responses found in Pury et al. (2007). However, in the event that some types of courage are underrepresented in a particular class, a good point for discussion might be why those types were not listed by class members.

courage theory? This discussion can lead nicely into a discussion of the risk component of courage and the practical and ethical concerns that guide research design.

Alternative Activity—The Role of Fear and Courage as an Accolade Versus Courage as a Process: Before you begin, divide the class into two groups. Ask students in Group 1 to write "Self" at the top of their papers and write for 5 minutes using the basic prompt.

Ask students in Group 2 to write "Other" at the top of their paper and to write for 5 minutes using this prompt: *Describe a time you observed (either directly or indirectly) someone else acting courageously. What do think the person was thinking and feeling? Describe what you think led up to the action, the action itself, and the outcome of the action.*

After students have finished writing and switched stories, write two columns on the board: "Self" and "Other." Ask students to read the narratives they have been handed and to mark any phrases that indicate that the actor feels the emotional experience of fear. Then ask them to do the same for phrases about objective risk. Go around the room and ask each student whether he or she has a Self or Other narrative, and how much fear and risk were discussed in the narrative. Ask for examples from the narratives of fear and examples of risk. Explain the differences between process and accolade courage found in the Discussion. While Self narratives contain a mixture of process and accolade courage, Other narratives are typically exemplars of accolade courage. Thus, while both may have a high amount of risk, Self narratives should contain more fear.

This pair of prompts will generate narratives identical to those described above for the Self condition; narratives for the Other condition, of course, will be written from a third-person perspective and may differ in other ways. If this prompt is combined with any of the activities above, the distinction between Self and Other narratives can also be discussed. For example, in the types of courage activity, more exemplars of proto-typical physical courage and fewer exemplars psychological courage are likely to be given in the Other condition.

DISCUSSION   Courage research is in its infancy and at a descriptive phase. Much of the research conducted to date has used similar narrative methodology. I have tried this exercise and each of the variations with both advanced undergraduate positive psychology classes and a multilevel honors seminar on fear and courage. Not surprisingly, students provide narratives that are strikingly similar to those provided by undergraduate research samples. A brief conceptual overview of each area is discussed next.

Types of Courageous Acts: One of the first and most interesting dissociations that can be made about courageous actions is that they tend to fall into recognizable categories. Lopez, O'Byrne, and Petersen (2003) described the major distinctions between types of courage, two of which have been widely discussed. The first, *physical courage*, involves acting despite personal physical danger; for example, saving someone from drowning by diving into rough surf after them or pulling someone from a burning building. Two well-known U.S. awards for valor, the Medal of Honor for military personnel and the Carnegie Medal, celebrate this kind of courage.

The second type of courage commonly discussed, *moral courage*, involves doing what is right despite social opposition. Standing up to others for what you believe is right is a typical form of moral courage.

The third type of courage discussed by Lopez et al. (2003) is *vital courage,* or pushing beyond a struggle with an illness or other personally limiting factor to do something great. Vital courage appears to be a special case of Putman's (2004) broader idea of *psychological courage,* or facing psychological discomfort to pursue a meaningful goal. Typical acts of psychological courage include getting needed mental health treatment and taking on an intimidating task that one might fail.

Defining Features: The major features of all types of courageous action have been discussed for centuries in philosophical literature (see Putman, 2004, for a review). Beginning with these definitions, Rate (2010) described three main features: "(a) a willing, intentional act (b) involving substantial danger, difficulty, or risk to the actor (c) primarily motivated to bring about a noble good or morally worthy purpose" (p. 62).

Role of Fear in Courage as an Accolade Versus in Courage as a Process: The above three features, according to Rate (2010), might occur despite the presence of fear, but might not. The optional nature of fear in his approach stands in direct opposition to more behavioral conceptions of courage proposed by Rachman (1990) and currently exemplified by Norton and Weiss (2009). In the behavioral approach, courage only exists as action that occurs despite fear. Typically, studies involving courage-as-acting-despite-fear do not consider the goal of the action.

One of the primary distinctions in courage research is between studies that examine courage as an accolade and courage as a process (Pury & Starkey, 2010; see also the distinction between personal and general courage in Pury et al., 2007). Accolade courage includes actions that are praised by others or even by the actor as courageous for anyone. They are actions in which the risks are particularly high and the goals remarkably noble. By definition, all courageous actions cited by public awards for courage represent this type. Studies of accolade courage may or may not include fear as a part of courage—what seems to matter is observed risk and nobility of the goal. Process courage, on the other hand, involves the process by which someone takes an action for a noble good despite risk. That process can occur for actions that incur a wide range of risks and goals, from those universally agreed-on (fear of death, goal of saving a life) to highly personalized risks and goals (such as the fear of a spider or demonstrating a particular skill). These actions are likely to include fear as a part of courage and are commonly, but not always, in the behaviorist tradition (see also Norton & Weiss, 2009; Pury et al., 2007).

Role of Success in Accolade Courage: Actions labeled *courageous* in retrospect are typically those actions in which the noble goal was met. Awards for valor are typically made to those who succeed (or who die trying: see Pury & Starkey, 2010). Actions that succeed are seen as more courageous than actions that fail, even among individuals who state that intention, not outcome, is what matters for courage (Pury & Hensel, 2010).

CONCLUSION

This simple, in-class exercise gets students to think about courage in their own lives. It also helps them to make a direct connection between research findings and actions they have either taken themselves or observed. As new findings on courage are discovered, many of them may be folded in to this exercise by additions to or modifications of the basic prompt.[2]

---

[2]To better grasp this topic, instructors and students are encouraged to consult the following sources: Lopez et al. (2003); Pury et al. (2007); Pury and Starkey (2010); Putman (2004); Rachman (1990); and Rate (2010).

REFERENCES

Lopez, S. J., O'Byrne, K., & Petersen, S. (2003). Profiling courage. In S. J. Lopez & C. R. Snyder (Eds.), *Positive psychological assessment: A handbook of models and measures* (pp. 185–197). Washington, DC: American Psychological Association. doi:10.1037/10612-012.

Norton, P. J., & Weiss, B. J. (2009). The role of courage on behavioral approach in a fear-eliciting situation: A proof-of-concept pilot study. *Journal of Anxiety Disorders, 23*, 212–217. doi:10.1016/j.janxdis.2008.07.002

Pury, C. L. S., & Hensel, A. D. (2010). Are courageous actions successful actions? *The Journal of Positive Psychology, 5*(1), 62–72. doi:10.1080/17439760903435224

Pury, C. L. S., Kowalski, R. M., & Spearman, M. J. (2007). Distinctions between general and personal courage. *The Journal of Positive Psychology, 2*, 99–114. doi:10.1080/17439760701237962

Pury, C. L. S., & Starkey, C. B. (2010). Is courage an accolade or a process? A fundamental question for courage research. In C. L. S. Pury & S. J. Lopez (Eds.), *The psychology of courage: Modern research on an ancient virtue* (pp. 67–87). Washington, DC: American Psychological Association. doi:10.1037/12168-004

Putman, D. (2004). *Psychological courage.* Dallas, TX: University Press of America.

Rachman, S. (1990). *Fear and courage* (2nd ed.). New York, NY: Freeman.

Rate, C. R. (2010). Defining the features of courage: A search for meaning. In C. L. S. Pury & S. J. Lopez (Eds.), *The psychology of courage: Modern research on an ancient virtue* (pp. 47–66). Washington, DC: American Psychological Association. doi:10.1037/12168-003

2

HUMILITY
HUMILITY, THE MODEST STRENGTH
Robert A. Emmons

This chapter describes an activity centered on the strength of humility. Participants are encouraged to draw on a model of relational humility and think about the most humble person they know and then answer a series of questions about that person.

CONCEPT

Does humility matter? In contemporary society, it is easy to overlook humility's potential merits. In politics, business, and sports, the egoists command our attention. "Show me someone without an ego," said real estate mogul Donald Trump, "and I'll show you a loser." In contrast, contemporary research reveals that the unassuming virtue of humility, rather than representing weakness or inferiority, as is commonly assumed, is a strength of character that produces beneficial results for self and society. Humble people tend to be successful across life domains, particularly in the arena of relationships. One study found that humility was the characteristic most admired in lawyers, and another study found that humility was a predictor of teaching effectiveness among high school teachers (Tangney, 2009).

Although most traits can be measured by having people rate themselves, researchers have doubted the validity of self-reports of humility. That is, people who claim to be very humble would seem to be bragging about their humility, something truly humble people would not do. Researchers have hypothesized that to the degree that people are truly humble, they will more modestly report their own humility on self-report measures. Therefore, truly humble people may *modestly underreport* their humility, moderately humble people may *to some extent* overestimate their humility, and people low in humility (e.g., narcissists) may overestimate their humility *a great deal*. This challenge led Worthington (2007) to conclude that "asking a respondent to rate how humble he or she is is an exercise in futility" (p. ix). Given the problems with self-reports, researchers have sought other strategies of measuring humility.

MATERIALS NEEDED

Each student will need multiple copies of the single-page questionnaire (see Appendix 2.1), and two to three sheets of blank lined paper.

INSTRUCTIONS

Communicate to your students that there is no simple definition of *humility* but that it seems to involve the following elements: a clear and accurate (not underestimated) sense of one's abilities and achievements; the ability to acknowledge one's mistakes, imperfections, gaps in knowledge, and limitations; an openness to new ideas, contra-

---

DOI: 10.1037/14042-003

Activities for Teaching Positive Psychology: A Guide for Instructors, J. J. Froh and A. C. Parks (Editors)

dictory information, and advice; keeping one's abilities and accomplishments in perspective; a relatively low self-focus or an ability to "forget the self"; and appreciation of the value of all things, as well as the many different ways that people and things can contribute to our world.

Humility is intellectual and relational (Davis, Worthington, & Hook, 2010). *Intellectual humility* refers to having an accurate view of self—not too high or low (Tangney, 2009). In research, this has been measured as self-enhancement, which is the degree to which a person has an overly positive view of self. The *relational* aspect of humility includes interpersonal qualities such as respect and empathy during conflict, openness toward different cultures or worldviews, and exhibiting modesty in social interactions (e.g., deflecting attention away from oneself, showing interest in others, not bragging about one's accomplishments). Judgments of humble exemplars tend to take both features of humility into account.

This relational approach relies on observer judgments of target other persons (Davis et al., 2010). According to the relational approach, humility is best thought about and measured within a relationship and as a judgment of the humility in a target other person. Ask students to nominate the most or least humble person they have known. Ask them to think about "a person who you see as being very humble" (Exline & Geyer, 2004, p. 101). This may be someone with whom they are in a relationship or someone whom they have never met. They can then be asked further questions that capture the reasons why he or she is seen as humble, other qualities likely to be found in this person, and situations in which his or her humility was revealed. Then, have students rate the target person with the 16 items from the Relational Humility Scale (RHS; Davis et al., 2011), shown in Appendix 2.1. The RHS has three subscales: Global Humility, Superiority, and Self-Awareness.

After they have rated the individual on the RHS, ask students to spend 15 minutes writing about how the person they picked illustrates various aspects of humility. In what ways has the target person demonstrated humility in his or her words or actions? Is the humble exemplar known more for his or her relational humility, intellectual humility, or both? In what ways would you want to be more like the person you have chosen? Do you think that the person actively tries to be humble, or is humility just a fundamental way of being for them? Each of these questions is designed to stimulate a deeper appreciation of the nature of humility in everyday life. Depending on the size of the class, place students into groups of three or four. Then have them share their exemplars with the other members of the group, and have them discuss why they selected the person that they did. A spokesperson for each small group can then report to the entire class what was learned from the activity.

DISCUSSION   Challenges in measuring humility lead to a need for creative and indirect exercises for cultivating humility in the classroom. The activity described can be easily incorporated into classroom settings, and it provides a way of examining aspects of humility that will enable students to take a fresh look at this timeless virtue. The activity described represents a tried-and-true technique for stimulating an awareness of humility and opening the door to a consideration of the role of humility in creating a meaningful, fulfilling life.

A number of interesting questions designed to probe various aspects of the activity can be asked. For example, students can be asked whether their views of humility have changed as a consequence of engaging in the activity. They can be asked to reflect on why humility is a characteristic of effective teachers or may be effective in other occupations. They can be asked if they would prefer friends and romantic partners who display humility and if they can recall instances when a lack of humility in themselves or others led to problems in relationships. For the latter, they could be asked why it can be so difficult to live humbly. Are there personal or cultural forces that undermine humility? Finally, students should be asked to consider when humility might be a weakness rather than a strength and possible downsides of being too humble.[1]

REFERENCES Davis, D. E., Hook, J. N., Worthington, E. L., Jr., Van Tongeren, D. R., Gartner, A. L., Jennings, D. J., & Emmons, R. A. (2011). Relational humility: Conceptualizing and measuring humility as a personality judgment. *Journal of Personality Assessment, 93*, 225–234. doi:10.1080/00223891.2011.558871

Davis, D. E., Worthington, Jr., E. L., & Hook, J. N. (2010). Humility: Review of measurement strategies and conceptualization as personality judgment. *The Journal of Positive Psychology, 5*, 243–252. doi:10.1080/17439761003791672

Exline, J. J., & Geyer, A. L. (2004). Perceptions of humility: A preliminary investigation. *Self and Identity, 3*, 95–114. doi:10.1080/13576500342000077

Tangney, J. P. (2009). Humility. In S. J. Lopez & C. R. Snyder (Eds.), *Oxford handbook of positive psychology* (2nd ed., pp. 483–490). New York, NY: Oxford University Press.

Worthington, E. L. (2007). *Humility: The quiet virtue.* West Conshohocken, PA: Templeton Press.

---

[1]To better grasp this topic, instructors and students are encouraged to consult the following sources: Davis et al. (2010); Tangney (2009); Worthington (2007).

Appendix 2.1

The Relational Humility Scale

Instructions: Rate the person you have identified on the following statements, where 1 = *completely disagree* and 5 = *completely agree*.

He/she has a humble character. (GH)
He or she is truly a humble person. (GH)
Most people would consider him/her a humble person. (GH)
His or her close friends would consider him/her humble. (GH)
Even strangers would consider him/her humble. (GH)
He/she thinks of him/herself too highly. (S)
He/she has a big ego. (S)
He/she thinks of him/herself as overly important. (S)
Certain tasks are beneath him/her. (S)
I feel inferior when I am with him/her. (S)
He/she strikes me as self-righteous. (S)
He/she does not like doing menial tasks for others. (S)
He/she knows him/herself well. (SA)
He/she knows his/her strengths. (SA)
He/she knows his/her weaknesses. (SA)
He/she is self-aware. (SA)

Note. GH = Global Humility; S = Superiority; SA = Self-Awareness.

STRENGTHS
USING A STRENGTHS APPROACH TO BUILD
PERSPECTIVE-TAKING CAPACITY
Michelle C. Louis

This small-group activity challenges students to engage in perspective taking by adopting the "voice" of various strengths or themes of talent in response to several scenarios.

CONCEPT

Perspective taking, the ability to imagine a situation from another person's point of view, is widely regarded as a critical skill for managing interpersonal conflict and fostering positive social relationships (Galinsky, Ku, & Wang, 2005). The exercise in this chapter is designed to enhance students' ability to use a strengths approach to engage in perspective taking. It prompts reflection on how others' thoughts, feelings, and behaviors may be connected to the tendencies represented in their personal strengths assessment results and facilitates the process of reframing situations from alternative viewpoints.

The activity in this chapter is designed with the recognition that there are two prevalent models in contemporary understandings of strengths. One paradigm describes strengths as elements of *character* that produce virtue, whereas the other views strengths as personal *competencies* that generate optimal performance. Specifically, the Values in Action Institute conceptualizes *strengths* as morally valued components of character that contribute to a fulfilling life (Peterson & Seligman, 2004); the relative potency of 24 strengths is measured by using a free online survey called the Values in Action Inventory of Strengths (VIA-IS; Seligman, Park, & Peterson, 2004), or simply the VIA Survey.[1] Peterson (2006) noted that character strengths can be differentiated from talents on the basis that the former are morally valued in their own right whereas the latter are valued for the tangible consequences they produce. Alternatively, Gallup (1999) offers an online measure called the Clifton StrengthsFinder[2] to rank the prevalence of 34 *talent themes,* which are clusters of related thought, feeling, or behavior that can be applied in constructive ways. According to this framework, strengths result when knowledge and

---

[1]The Values in Action Institute offers the VIA Survey and corresponding strengths profile at no charge, available at http://www.viacharacter.org/Surveys/SurveyCenter.aspx.

[2]The Clifton StrengthsFinder requires the purchase of an online access code, available at http://www.strengthsquest.com/purchase. Gallup, *Clifton StrengthsFinder,* and *the Clifton Strengths Finder* theme names are trademarks of Gallup, Inc. All rights reserved.

DOI: 10.1037/14042-004

Activities for Teaching Positive Psychology: A Guide for Instructors, J. J. Froh and A. C. Parks (Editors)

skill refine existing talent, producing "consistent, near-perfect performance in a given activity" (Buckingham & Clifton, 2001, p. 42).

The VIA Survey measures character strengths, whereas the Clifton StrengthsFinder measures talent themes that are the building blocks of strength. The language used throughout this chapter captures this subtle difference in the nature of the assessment results provided by each instrument while remaining inclusive of both. The authors of these instruments encourage a focus on the top five results provided by their respective inventory, whether the five "signature strengths" (VIA-IS) or the five "signature themes" (Clifton StrengthsFinder), as these high-ranking descriptors indicate an individual's dominant personal tendencies. Although other strengths assessments exist, this chapter highlights the Clifton StrengthsFinder and the VIA Survey as they are commonly used in postsecondary settings. The exercise in this chapter is relevant whether a class is working with VIA's character-based strengths classification, Gallup's competency-oriented model, or both.

MATERIALS
NEEDED

Students will need the printed results of their completed strengths assessment, whether the VIA-IS or the Clifton StrengthsFinder. Although it is not required, preparation of printed handouts that provide a brief description of all of the strengths or talent themes measured by whichever assessment students have taken may be helpful.[3] A projection screen or chalkboard is also needed for posting a series of discussion questions. For the writing component, print instructions for students or create an alternative plan for making the assignment guidelines available.

INSTRUCTIONS

The activity in this chapter requires that students have a solid understanding of their own strengths assessment results as well as a working knowledge of the other strengths or themes identified by the assessment you are using. The activity will work best if you have previously devoted some class time to discussing the meaning of various strengths or talent themes and when students have done some reading or in-class activities related to this topic.

To begin, read (or paraphrase) the statements in the following paragraph:

> Signature strengths/talent themes often represent the "lens" through which people view the world. This lens influences the things people value or find important in a situation, the kinds of questions they tend to ask, the information they focus on, and the emotions they experience, all of which can shape their behavior. Understanding others' core strengths/talent themes can provide some insight into how they view a situation and why they might respond to it as they do.

Tell students that you will be offering them some situations to consider. They will not be asked about how they would personally respond to each scenario. Instead, they will be asked to view the scenario through the lens of an assigned strength or

---

[3]Brief descriptions of all 24 character strengths identified by the VIA-IS can be accessed by clicking *View Full Report* upon completion of the assessment, and an overview of each of the 34 Clifton StrengthsFinder talent themes can be found online at http://www.strengthsquest.com/content/141365/Resources.aspx, by clicking on the link labeled *Theme Quick Reference Card.*

talent theme. By considering the situation from that perspective, their task is to become the "voice" of their designated strength/theme in response to several questions. Ask the students to number off by fours, and then instruct those with the same number to situate themselves together in each of the four quadrants of the classroom. Next, designate each of the four groups as responsible for representing a different strength/theme. Predetermine which strengths/themes you plan to use for this exercise, as some may lend themselves more readily to certain scenarios than others and therefore may enable students to engage with the exercise more easily. Some sample scenarios and suggested strengths/themes to accompany each are provided in Appendix 3.1.

Begin by announcing a situation such as "preparing a group presentation for a class." Then, ask each group to discuss the following questions posted on the screen:

- What might be the *priorities* or *goals* of someone with your strength/theme in this situation?
- Which *questions* might someone with your assigned strength/theme tend to ask in this situation?
- What might a person with this strength/theme *do* in this situation?

Ask any other questions that you believe might apply to the situation you have selected. Give the class several minutes to discuss these items within their groups and instruct them to brainstorm multiple responses for each question if they are able to do so. Then, open the discussion to the full class, giving each group an opportunity to "be the voice" of its strength/theme. In the event that a group has difficulty generating a response, ask the rest of the students to offer ideas. In some cases, it may be helpful for you to ask the students to clarify why they believe that a particular response would be associated with their assigned strength or theme. Repeat the activity as desired, assigning the groups a new strength/theme for each scenario so that students can practice shifting perspectives.

DISCUSSION   Students commonly report that exposure to the results of a strengths assessment is a meaningful, affirming experience. They gain a concrete vocabulary for describing their positive qualities, and they emerge with a deeper understanding of their unique values and skills. Increasing students' self-awareness is beneficial, and yet when the strengths conversation ends there, it can assume a somewhat egocentric tone. The activity in this chapter is derived from the notion that strengths development encompasses more than understanding and nurturing one's personal qualities; it also entails cultivating an appreciation for others and valuing differing perspectives.

Although focusing solely on one strength or theme obscures the reality that these qualities do not exist in isolation, I have found that students are initially better able to engage the exercise when asked to consider the influence of one specific strength/theme instead of several at a time. When students become more proficient at viewing situations through the lens of different strengths or themes, you might then proceed by asking students to consider *combinations* of strengths or talents as they respond to a specific situation. One way to do so is to present a hypothetical signature profile of five strengths or talent themes along with specific questions that help students process how the elements of the profile might interact. For example, I might provide a profile accompanied by a general scenario such as "looking for a new job" and ask the class questions such as the following:

- What might a person with this profile desire in a supervisor?
- Which features of a work environment might be important to a person with this profile?
- What might characterize the working style of someone with this profile?

This type of activity provides an ideal backdrop for discussing not only how strengths or themes combine together but also how they interact with environmental contexts and myriad personal factors to produce unique expressions between individuals. This conversation provides an opportunity to remind students that a person's signature profile does not definitively reveal how that individual will respond in a given scenario; instead it offers initial clues for further exploration.

The scenarios provided in this chapter are intended to be generally applicable for traditionally aged undergraduate students, but they can be easily modified according to the nature of the course in which they are embedded. For example, in teaching a course on organizational leadership, I designed scenarios on issues pertinent to that specific topic, such as decision making, work styles, team dynamics, and conflict. The scenarios in Appendix 3.1 are therefore not intended to be prescriptive but are instead offered as descriptive examples.

WRITING COMPONENT

This writing component can be assigned for students to complete after class as a way to personalize and reinforce the use of a strengths approach in perspective taking. Give students the following directions for an essay: Write about a specific situation in your life in which you and someone you know well (a roommate, coworker, parent, friend, or significant other) approached a situation with different priorities or from two seemingly distinct perspectives. Describe the scenario in enough detail to give the reader a solid overview of how both you and the other person reacted to the situation. Then, indicate which of your signature strengths or themes influenced how you approached the situation, describing how your thoughts, statements, or behaviors might have been shaped by those particular strengths/themes. Next, consider which strengths/themes might have informed the other person's response. Even if you do not know the other person's signature profile, try to reframe the situation to view it from his or her perspective. Your goal is to construct a logical argument that explains the other person's response, and doing so may require that you guess which strengths/themes are dominant for that person on the basis of the opinions or priorities he or she expressed to you. Finally, reflect on the impact this exercise had on your understanding of the situation. Describe how using a strengths approach to reframe a situation might help you when you encounter people whose perspectives differ from your own.[4]

---

[4]To better grasp this topic, instructors and students are encouraged to consult the following sources: Clifton, Anderson, and Schreiner (2006); Peterson (2006); Peterson and Park (2009).

REFERENCES

Buckingham, M., & Clifton, D. O. (2001). *Now, discover your strengths.* New York, NY: Free Press.

Clifton, D. O., Anderson, C. E., & Schreiner, L. A. (2006). *StrengthsQuest: Discover and develop your strengths in academics, career, and beyond* (2nd ed.). New York, NY: Gallup Press.

Galinsky, A. D., Ku, G., & Wang, C. S. (2005). Perspective-taking and self-other overlap: Fostering social bonds and facilitating social coordination. *Group Processes & Intergroup Relations, 8,* 109–124. doi:10.1177/1368430205051060

Gallup. (1999). *Clifton StrengthsFinder.* Washington, DC: Author.

Peterson, C. (2006). Character strengths. In C. Peterson (Ed.), *A primer in positive psychology* (pp. 137–164). New York, NY: Oxford University Press.

Peterson, C., & Park, N. (2009). Classifying and measuring strengths of character. In S. J. Lopez & C. R. Snyder (Eds.), *Oxford handbook of positive psychology* (2nd ed., pp. 25–33). New York, NY: Oxford University Press.

Peterson, C., & Seligman, M. E. P. (2004). *Character strengths and virtues: A handbook and classification.* Washington, DC, and New York, NY: American Psychological Association and Oxford University Press.

Seligman, M. E. P., Park, N., & Peterson, C. (2004). The Values in Action (VIA) classification of character strengths. *Ricerche di Psicologia, 27,* 63–78.

Appendix 3.1

Sample Scenarios and Suggested Talent Themes
or Character Strengths

As described in the chapter, give each of four groups of students the name of a different talent theme or character strength. Ideas for possible scenarios followed by suggested talent themes (Clifton StrengthsFinder) or character strengths (VIA-IS) to assign to each group are provided in the left and right boxes, respectively.

Scenario 1: Preparing a Group Presentation for a Class

Relator Arranger Maximizer Input	Zest Judgment and open-mindedness Perseverance Creativity

Scenario 2: First Week on Campus as a Student at Your College or University

Woo	Appreciation for beauty and excellence
Context	Leadership
Includer	Love of learning
Discipline	Self-regulation

Scenario 3: Working Through a Conflict With a Significant Other

	Humor
Harmony	Curiosity
Command	Prudence and discretion
Empathy	Kindness

Scenario 4: Leading Members of an Athletic Team as Their Captain

Futuristic	Modesty and humility
Consistency	Gratitude
Individualization	Fairness
Developer	Hope

4

EUDAIMONIA
CONTRASTING TWO CONCEPTIONS OF HAPPINESS: HEDONIA AND EUDAIMONIA
Alan S. Waterman

Hedonia and eudaimonia are two conceptions of happiness whose roots can be traced to classical Hellenic philosophy. The teaching exercise described here uses the Personally Expressive Activities Questionnaire to demonstrate differences in their implications for positive psychological functioning.

CONCEPT

The nature of happiness, its sources, and its promotion have become major themes within positive psychology. This exercise explores two conceptions of happiness: *hedonia* (happiness as pleasure) and *eudaimonia* (happiness as personal fulfillment). Among the aspects explored are how each is experienced subjectively, their sources in various types of activities, and the relationship between them.

MATERIALS NEEDED

The exercise involves having students complete a brief version of the Personally Expressive Activities Questionnaire (Waterman, 2011), specifically adapted for teaching purposes. The questionnaire appears in Appendix 4.1.

INSTRUCTIONS

Within the field of positive psychology an important distinction has been made between hedonic and eudaimonic functioning. This distinction can be traced back to classical Hellenic philosophy, most notably to Aristotle (4th Century BCE/1985) in the *Nicomachean Ethics*. In ethical theory, *hedonism* involves considering happiness, understood as pleasure, to be the primary, if not necessarily the sole good worth pursuing. In contrast, eudaimonia, usually translated as happiness, focuses on the good life as one involving activity expressing virtue, where virtue is considered the best within us or excellence (Haybron, 2008; Kraut, 1979). Aristotle (1985) emphatically rejected hedonism as a goal in life: "The many, the most vulgar, seemingly conceive the good and happiness as pleasure, and hence they also like the life of gratification. Here they appear completely slavish, since the life they decide on is a life for grazing animals" (p. 7).

Within psychology, the distinction between hedonic and eudaimonic functioning has been studied on several levels: (a) as conceptions of well-being; (b) as motivation, that is, the type of goals to be pursued; and (c) as subjective experiences accompanying differing types of activities (Ryan & Deci, 2001). The exercise described here is based on contrasting two conceptions of happiness as subjective states accompanying activities.

DOI: 10.1037/14042-005
Activities for Teaching Positive Psychology: A Guide for Instructors, J. J. Froh and A. C. Parks (Editors)

Hedonic enjoyment, or hedonia,[1] refers to subjective experiences of pleasure we experience when we engage in activities that we enjoy doing. In contrast, eudaimonia, as a set of subjective experiences, refers to how we feel when engaged in activities that involve personal fulfillment, that is, the expression of our best potentials (Norton, 1976). The constellation of experiences associated with self-realization includes feelings of immediate positive connection with an activity on the first occasion it is engaged in; a sense of rightness and centeredness in one's actions; strength of purpose; meaningfulness; intrinsic motivation; fulfillment; personal expressiveness; and identity, as in "this is who I really am."

The distinction between hedonia and eudaimonia is used to make the point that the source of happiness (i.e., the activity, event, or circumstance giving rise to happiness) makes a difference with respect to how happiness is experienced. Eudaimonia is experienced when the activities engaged in reflect the expression of our personal potentials. It is also clearly true that we typically enjoy engaging in such activities, so it can be said that eudaimonia and hedonia are experienced concurrently. However, we enjoy a wide variety of activities that do not entail utilization of our best potentials, for example, having a good meal, going to a movie or concert, or doing something that earns us money or praise. For such activities, hedonia would be said to be present, but not experiences of eudaimonia. And it is certainly true that many activities in which we engage do not generate experiences of either hedonia or eudaimonia. Correlations between measures of hedonia and eudaimonia for identity-related activities are typically very strong, in the range of .75 to .85. Despite that strong association, correlations between eudaimonia and measures of variables such as involvement of one's best potentials, level of challenge, level of effort, and importance have consistently been found to be significantly stronger than the corresponding correlations with hedonia (Waterman, 2011; Waterman, Schwartz, & Conti, 2008).

It is essential to emphasize Norton's (1976) point that experiencing eudaimonia should not be considered the goal of a good life. Rather, it is an indicator that what individuals are doing is concordant with their best personal potentials. Such experiences are an integral part of identity formation, the means by which better identity choices can be recognized. As the ethical philosophy of eudaimonism conveys, the goal in living is not positive subjective experiences of eudaimonia but rather the objective condition of eudaimonia, that is, bringing forth the best within us through the actualization of our potentials.

The exercise described here is structured in three parts: (a) a questionnaire to be completed in class, (b) a class discussion, and (c) a written assignment. The purpose of the exercise is to introduce students to the distinction between hedonia and eudaimonia and to help them to recognize the type of activities that give rise to the differing types of subjective experiences.

The questionnaire should be completed before students are provided with descriptions of the two conceptions of happiness. Otherwise, advance knowledge may color

---

[1]The term *hedonia* is of modern origin. It was introduced as a term to connote subjective experiences of happiness, as pleasure, that would function on the same level as subjective experiences of eudaimonia.

the students' responses. It is preferable to have the questionnaire completed in class so that the instructor can respond to questions the students may have. However, an alternative would be to have students complete the questionnaire outside of class.

The Personally Expressive Activities Questionnaire (see Appendix 4.1) is a flexible instrument with respect to the types of activities to be rated. In this exercise, I have proposed using projected work and leisure activities as the basis of comparison. However, the questions are applicable to almost any type of activity in which students engage or in which they might engage at some subsequent time. Instructors might wish to substitute other activities for projected work and leisure, for example, activities that are "competitive and cooperative," "religious and secular," or "by oneself and with other people." If other types of activities are used in the exercise, the instructions should be rewritten accordingly.

For this exercise, students should be asked to think of what type of work they would like to be engaged in 3 to 5 years after completing their education. If they do not have specific career plans, they should think of some type of work they might enjoy. Next, they should think of what type of leisure activity they would like to be engaged in 3 to 5 years after completing their education. Students should write down both their projected work and their projected leisure activities.

The instructor should then distribute two copies of the questionnaire to each student. One sheet should be labeled *Projected Work Activity* and the other *Projected Leisure Activity*. After completing the questionnaire, students should be provided with descriptions of hedonia and eudaimonia (labeled *H* and *E* on the questionnaire) and asked to look at the H and E items with a view to seeing their relevance for each conception of happiness. They should then calculate their own hedonia and eudaimonia scores for both types of activities. If class time permits, actual means for eudaimonia and hedonia for each type of activity can be generated, though a faster and simpler procedure would be to ask students to raise their hands under the following circumstances: (a) Were their eudaimonia scores for projected work higher than, lower than, or equal to their eudaimonia scores for projected leisure? and (b) Were their hedonia scores for projected work higher than, lower than, or equal to their hedonia scores for projected leisure? It would normally be expected that eudaimonia scores will be higher for work than for leisure whereas hedonia scores will be higher for leisure than for work (though this may vary by the student's year in school and field of anticipated work activity).

DISCUSSION

After the scores are generated, a class discussion should be held focusing on what the H and E items appear to have in common and how they differ. The similarities of experiences of eudaimonia to flow and peak experiences are worth noting, if students are familiar with those concepts. The discussion can then shift to what it is about activities that gives rise to experiences of hedonia and eudaimonia. At this point, the relationship between experiences of eudaimonia and activities involving a person's best potentials should be discussed.

The question of the relationship between the two conceptions of happiness should be raised, if not by a student then by the instructor. Elizabeth Telfer (1980), a philosopher, claimed that eudaimonia is a sufficient but not a necessary condition for experiences of hedonic enjoyment. This means that particular activities in which a person might engage will give rise to both eudaimonia and hedonia; other sources of happiness are enjoyed in the hedonic sense without concurrent eudaimonia being present. If students are unclear about the rationale for the placement of items on the hedonic enjoyment and eudaimonia scales, remind the class that there is an expected strong correlation between the two scales, although research evidence indicates that they have discriminant validity. The items on the hedonic enjoyment scale all refer to a positive emotional state (e.g., enjoyment, pleasure), which corresponds to the presence of hedonia alone. In contrast, all of the items on the eudaimonia scale include a reference to feeling a special connection with the activity being rated (e.g., who I really am, what I was meant to do), which corresponds to the concurrent presence of eudaimonia and hedonia. It is also worth discussing whether eudaimonia indeed is always accompanied by experiences of hedonia. Can the students think of any circumstances under which a person would experience eudaimonia (considered as feelings of personal expressiveness) but not necessarily enjoy what is being done?

Whereas Aristotle associated eudaimonia with expressions of virtue, another topic for discussion is whether eudaimonia as a subjective condition could be experienced during engagement in an unethical activity, such as pulling off a clever jewelry heist. What implications follow from recognizing that eudaimonia could arise from both ethical and unethical behaviors?

WRITING COMPONENT

The final part of this exercise is a written assignment. To set this up, students should be informed that scores of 36 and above should be considered high on eudaimonia, and similarly for hedonia. Scores between 13 and 35 should be considered moderate, and scores of 12 and below should be considered low. The writing assignment should have students address the following questions:

- What does the pattern of your scores concerning eudaimonia and hedonia in the areas of your projected work and leisure activities tell you about how you see your future?
- Does this have you feeling comfortable or uncomfortable? Why?
- If this exercise has left you feeling uncomfortable, what do you believe you may need to do to make you feel more comfortable about your future?

Past experience with the scales for eudaimonia and hedonia suggests that few students will generate scores on either scale of 12 or below for work or for leisure (virtually never for leisure; very seldom for work). Should the pattern of the students' responses to the scales have them feeling uncomfortable, reassurance can be provided in almost all instances in that their numbers are at least in the moderate range, if this is indeed the case. Students scoring in the low range on these measures would be well-advised to seek counseling because such numbers suggest that their lives are not going well. (For such students, this exercise will not be providing them with any information that they do not already know about themselves.)[2]

---

[2]To better grasp this topic, instructors and students are encouraged to consult the following sources: Kraut (1979); Ryan and Deci (2001); and Waterman (2011).

REFERENCES

Aristotle. (1985). *Nicomachean ethics.* (T. Irwin, Trans.). Indianapolis, IN: Hackett. (Original work 4th Century B.C.E.)

Haybron, D. M. (2008). *The pursuit of unhappiness: The elusive psychology of well-being.* New York, NY: Oxford University Press.

Kraut, R. (1979). Two conceptions of happiness. *The Philosophical Review, 88,* 167–196. doi:10.2307/2184505

Norton, D. L. (1976). *Personal destinies: A philosophy of ethical individualism.* Princeton, NJ: Princeton University Press.

Ryan, R. M., & Deci, E. L. (2001). On happiness and human potentials: A review of research on hedonic and eudaimonic well-being. *Annual Review of Psychology, 52,* 141–166. doi:10.1146/annurev.psych.52.1.141

Telfer, E. (1980). *Happiness.* New York, NY: St. Martin's Press.

Waterman, A. S. (2011). Eudaimonic identity theory: Identity as self-discovery. In S. J. Schwartz, K. Luyckx, & V. L. Vignoles (Eds.), *Handbook of identity theory and research* (pp. 357–379). New York, NY: Springer. doi:10.1007/978-1-4419-7988-9_16

Waterman, A. S., Schwartz, S. J., & Conti, R. (2008). The implications of two conceptions of happiness (hedonic enjoyment and eudaimonia) for the understanding of intrinsic motivation. *Journal of Happiness Studies, 9,* 41–79. doi:10.1007/s10902-006-9020-7

Appendix 4.1

Projected (Work) (Leisure) Activity: _____

For the items below, please use the following scale:

Strongly Disagree 1 2 3 4 5 6 7 Strongly Agree

Below are a series of statements regarding a variety of positive feelings that you anticipate may be present in varying degrees when engaging in projected (work) (leisure) activities. To what extent do you agree with each of the following statements:

_____ 1(E)   This activity will give me my greatest feeling of really being alive.
_____ 2(H)   When I engage in this activity I will feel more satisfied than I do when engaged in most other activities.
_____ 3(H)   This activity will give me my strongest sense of enjoyment.
_____ 4(E)   When I engage in this activity I will feel more intensely involved than I do when engaged in most other activities.
_____ 5(H)   When I engage in this activity I will feel good.
_____ 6(E)   This activity will give me my strongest feeling that this is who I really am.
_____ 7(E)   When I engage in this activity I will feel that this is what I was meant to do.
_____ 8(H)   This activity will give me my greatest pleasure.
_____ 9(H)   When I engage in this activity I will feel a warm glow.
_____ 10(E) I will feel more complete or fulfilled when engaging in this activity than I will when engaged in most other activities.
_____ 11(H) When I engage in this activity I will feel happier than I do when engaged in most other activities.
_____ 12(E) I will feel a special fit or meshing when engaging in this activity.

H Score _____ E Score _____

5

WORK
THE VALUE(S) OF WORK
Christopher Michaelson

This activity facilitates discussion and reflection on why we work and the value of work. Students inventory types of work, articulate and debate the intrinsic and instrumental value of work, and draw collective and individual conclusions about the value of the work they expect to do.

CONCEPT

If the good life has value, and work is necessary (in most cases) to life, then it seems that valuable work is often integral to the good life. However, different people relate to their work in different ways. Wrzesniewski, McCauley, Rozin, and Schwarz (1997) suggested that

> most people see their work as either a Job (focus on financial rewards and necessity rather than pleasure or fulfillment; not a major positive part of life), a Career (focus on advancement), or a Calling (focus on enjoyment of fulfilling, socially useful work). (p. 21)

The job-career-calling typology primarily leans toward examining the subjective experience of work, whereas Care (1984) leaned toward the objective responsibility of workers. Care suggested that two moral values are "in competition with one another" in the choice of one's career—self-realization (or self-determination) and service to others—and that when only one can be chosen in our world full of need, we have a moral obligation to choose service to others. This moral analysis does not fully account for another force, market fit, which Michaelson (2009) noted is not entirely within the subject's control yet also powerfully influences career choice. Even if there is a free market for work, we certainly do not have the freedom to choose any sort of work we want. There may be barriers to choosing valuable work, and thus to living the good life, that should be explored—institutional barriers (e.g., job requirements), individual barriers (e.g., insufficient ability), and other barriers (e.g., immediate economic needs interfering with longer term aspirations).

MATERIALS NEEDED

Paper, blackboard, and writing utensils are useful at a minimum, though you may also facilitate the discussion with and record results in PowerPoint (in class) or use survey tools to gather information (prior to class).

INSTRUCTIONS

Many students have an idea of the type of work they are preparing for but may not have thoughtfully considered why. These students, if pressed for a reason for their choice, might offer the prospect of making a decent living, or they might consider the type of

---

DOI: 10.1037/14042-006

work to be a good fit for their skill set or interests. Other students may not have any work-related plans. These students may have idealistic dreams of fulfilling, enriching work, or they may have no inspiring hopes at all that work could serve. Of course, most students will have mixed feelings about work and display a combination of these sentiments, although they have limited experience in thinking carefully about why they might do the work they will do. We all stand to benefit from reflection on why we work, because having a sense of purpose or meaning in one's work can influence job satisfaction and productivity, among other contributions to personal and social well-being (Care, 1984; Michaelson, 2009; Muirhead, 2004; Wrzesniewski et al., 1997).

Myriad types of work are necessary or desirable for the functioning of a society. If we consider a moderate-sized society, we imagine a variety of roles that people fill, from teaching to law enforcement, food service to financial services, entertainment to janitorial cleanup. As a class, discuss and ultimately inventory types of work typical of a society. The purpose is not so much to generate a comprehensive inventory of types of work but to craft an inventory that represents a generous variety of types of work (say, 20–30, depending on the length of your planned discussion), some of which the students themselves may be contemplating for their futures and others of which they might never have considered. A sample list might include the following:

- artist,
- bond trader,
- business executive,
- clergy,
- educator,
- nonprofit worker,
- panhandler,
- police officer,
- repair technician,
- administrative assistant,
- store clerk, and
- waiter.

Discuss the list as a whole with the class, eliciting comments on such topics as the variety of work there is in a typical society, the inputs (e.g., training, education) needed for different types of work, the outputs (e.g., salary, reputation) resulting from some types of work, segueing eventually into the value of certain work.

An optional but valuable activity to undertake in preparation for this discussion would be to read books or view films and discuss the value of work to key characters. For example, Alcott's (1873/1994) novel *Work* depicts the career path of a woman who sets out on her own willing to do nearly any kind of work to make ends meet and rises to become an advocate for women's rights in the workplace. Other literature about work includes the forlorn copyists of Gogol's (1842/1992) "The Overcoat" and Melville's (1853/2004) *Bartleby*, men who would today be replaced by machines. Chang (2008) provided a powerful journalistic account of the motivations of *Factory Girls*, who leave their rural villages for comparatively lucrative, though mundane, work in industrial cities. Other journalistic narratives that are valuable in discussion of this topic include *Portraits 9/11/01: Collected 'Portraits of Grief'* from the *New York Times* staff (2002), which provide glimpses into why victims of the 9/11 terrorist attacks were at work on that tragic day, and Terkel's (1974) *Working*, a classic collection of ordinary worker's accounts of "what they do all day and how they feel about what they do."

In view of the relative dearth of good narrative literature about work, viewing and discussing films in which work is a central theme can be a valuable individual or group preparation activity. Chang's 2007 documentary, *Up the Yangtze*, follows two teenagers' different paths to and motivations for leaving their families to work on Yangtze River cruises in an economically booming China. Lee's 1989 film, *Do the Right Thing*, shows the interplay between race and class in a pizzeria where the owner sees his work as a service to the economically depressed community, whereas his son professes to "detest" his work, "like a disease." In Bird's 2004 animated film, *The Incredibles*, superheroes are prevented from fulfilling their callings because of concerns about legal liability, demonstrating the potential intrinsic value of work to both self-realization and the opportunity to serve others.

There are two general reasons why work may have value. Within these two reasons lie various considerations, but the broad categories of value align with a traditional philosophical distinction between intrinsic and instrumental value (similar to the psychological distinction between intrinsic and extrinsic value and associated with the motivations to work). That which has intrinsic value is considered to be valuable as an end in itself, whereas that which has instrumental value is considered to be valuable as a means to a purposeful end. One (overly simplistic, though instructive) way to think about intrinsic and instrumental value as they relate to work is that intrinsically valuable work is work that you might perform for free, whereas instrumental value is measured by the compensation (material or otherwise) received for work performed. For example, the work of a civil rights activist might have high intrinsic value in the form of both self-realization and service to others, even though it may not be instrumentally well compensated.

In this part of the exercise, groups of three to five students will plot the types of work on the list on the matrix shown in Figure 5.1. Before the types of work can be plotted, students will need to define the terms of the discussion:

- What, by general agreement, is the dividing line between low and high intrinsic value? This can be a complex discussion and can cover multiple factors, including but not limited to self-realization and service to others.
- What, by general agreement, is the dividing line between low and high instrumental value? This discussion might be straightforward and quantifiable, but students should be encouraged to consider what, in addition to material compensation, makes work instrumentally valuable, including, for example, skills learned and job mobility.

Some factors might be difficult to characterize as intrinsically versus instrumentally valuable (e.g., fun). To help set these terms, students should be encouraged to define the axes so that about half of the work types will fall on each side of each line, so roughly one-quarter of the list will be plotted in each quadrant of the matrix (see Appendix 5.1 for a blank matrix). Of course, students may need to compromise on how to define the positions of the axes and how to plot the types of work, but discussing these challenges is part of the value of the exercise.

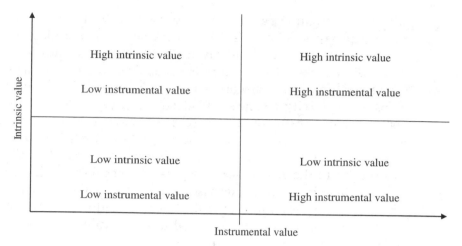

Figure 5.1. Intrinsic and instrumental value.

What does it all mean? You may ask students this question in regard to the results of the exercise, and students may ask this question in regard to the role of work in the good life. You should encourage students to explore not only the subjective experience of work that promotes self-realization but also the potential objective responsibility to do work that serves others.

Before discussing this question, you may also want to work with the full class to reconcile, if possible, competing definitions of *value* among the small groups and to determine which positions elicited broad agreement or disagreement about value. In the course of discussing what it all means, additional topics that might arise include the following:

- What does it take to obtain work that is both intrinsically and instrumentally valuable? (Often, competition for these positions is greater or barriers to entry are higher.)
- Why would anyone do work that is neither intrinsically nor instrumentally valuable? (Sometimes these positions are no less important than others, and someone has to do them, even if few truly want to and the market undervalues them.)
- What does this say about the free market for work? What does this say about social justice and employment? (Some students may idealistically suppose that they have significant market power, whereas others may be disappointed by the realization that obtaining their ideal job is not entirely within their control.)
- Is valuable work a moral obligation? Is valuable work a luxury item? (Some students may be adamant that work is a means to a large paycheck, whereas others may aspire to "meaningful" work without knowing whether it is possible.)
- If not every type of work can be valuable in both ways, is there a "break-even line" at which a compromise between intrinsic and instrumental value can be made? (The line might be perceived to run from the upper left-hand corner of the matrix to the lower right-hand corner. Above the line are positions that either reflect a healthy balance of intrinsic and instrumental value or that may have enough of one to compensate for the relative absence of the other. Below the line are positions that have a significant deficit of one, the other, or both.)

On closing, you may wish to encourage students to reflect on what they learned about themselves from the exercise. On the basis of their reflections, students should write a four- to six-page paper that reports on and analyzes the following topics:

- What type of work are you preparing for or considering preparing for and why (i.e., what is of value)?
- How do you define valuable work, and how might others challenge your definition?
- What is the role of valuable work in a good life?
- Is the good life a life that is just good for you? Good for others? Explain, and connect your answer to your statements about the work you are doing and why, how you define valuable work, and the role of work in a good life.[1]

REFERENCES

Alcott, L. M. (1994). *Work: A story of experience.* New York, NY: Penguin. (Original work published 1873)

Bird, B. (2004). *The incredibles* (Animated film). United States: Pixar.

Care, N. (1984). Career choice. *Ethics, 94,* 283–302. doi:10.1086/292533

Chang, L. T. (2008). *Factory girls: From village to city in a changing China.* New York, NY: Spiegel & Grau.

Chang, Y. (2007). *Up the Yangtze* (Documentary film). United States: Zeitgeist Films.

Gogol, N. (1992). The overcoat (I. F. Hapgood, Trans.). In S. Applebaum (Ed.), *The overcoat and other short stories* (pp. 79–103). Mineola, NY: Dover. (Original work published 1842)

Lee, S. (1989). *Do the right thing* (Film). United States: Universal Studios.

Melville, H. (2004). Bartleby, the scrivener. In W. Berthoff (Ed.), *Great short works of Herman Melville* (pp. 39–74). New York, NY: HarperCollins. (Original work published 1853)

Michaelson, C. (2009). Teaching meaningful work: Philosophical discussions on the ethics of career choice. *Journal of Business Ethics Education, 6,* 43–67.

Muirhead, R. (2004). *Just work.* Cambridge, MA: Harvard University Press.

New York Times staff (2002). *Portraits 9/11/01: The collected "portraits of grief" from the New York Times.* New York, NY: Times Books. Retrieved from http://www.nytimes.com/interactive/us/sept-11-reckoning/portraits-of-grief.html?8qa

Terkel, S. (1974). *Working: People talk about what they do all day and how they feel about what they do.* New York, NY: The New Press.

Wrzesniewski, A., McCauley, C., Rozin, P., & Schwarz, B. (1997). Jobs, careers, and callings: People's relations to their work. *Journal of Research in Personality, 31,* 21–33. doi:10.1006/jrpe.1997.2162

---

[1]To better grasp this topic, instructors and students are encouraged to consult the following sources: Alcott (1873/1994); Bird (2004); L. T. Chang (2008); Y. Chang (2007); Gogol (1842/1992); Lee (1989); Melville (1853/2004); *New York Times* staff (2002); Terkel (1974).

Appendix 5.1

Blank matrix (for reproduction and use)

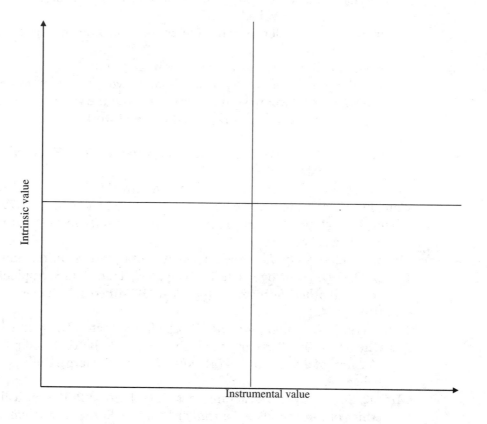

CULTURE AND IDENTITY
INTEGRATING AN UNDERSTANDING OF CULTURAL CONTEXT INTO A DISCUSSION OF POSITIVE TRAITS
Jennifer Teramoto Pedrotti

This exercise is designed to help students to see the influence of their personal culture on the cultivation of specific positive characteristics (e.g., courage, well-being, nurturance); this will then assist them in seeing how culture is relevant in the lives of others around them. A pair-share method is used to set up a larger group discussion of this topic.

CONCEPT

Culture is something that we must discuss in addressing any area of psychology, as no individual or group exists in a vacuum. To say what is "healthy" or "normal," one must consider the cultural context from which the judgment will be made. Cultural context is, in part, derived from our own personal cultural facets (e.g., race, ethnicity, gender) and can be a source of strength for us in developing specific positive characteristics (Pedrotti, 2011). This activity is designed to facilitate understanding of the role of culture in developing, cultivating, and interpreting these characteristics.

INSTRUCTIONS

In positive psychology, addressing cultural issues and contexts is essential in determining what is valued as a positive characteristic within a particular group. Researchers have argued that certain traits may be seen across all cultures, and many positive psychologists see a need to consider any personality characteristic as *culturally embedded* (Snyder, Lopez, & Pedrotti, 2011). Although all cultures have traits that they consider to be positive, and some traits may exist across various cultures, these constructs may be ranked differently depending on their cultural value and at the same time may be manifested in different ways (see Pedrotti, Edwards, & Lopez, 2009, for a more detailed description of these concepts).

Culture may be defined to include many different facets. While some definitions may include only identity facets such as race and ethnicity, others may include different salient factors in the life of the individual. Hays (2008) created a framework that uses the word ADDRESSING to discuss a broad, multifaceted definition of culture in counseling conceptualizations. In this exercise, the ADDRESSING framework can be used to assist us in understanding how complex the term culture can be.

DOI: 10.1037/14042-007
Activities for Teaching Positive Psychology: A Guide for Instructors, J. J. Froh and A. C. Parks (Editors)

Hays (2008) uses each of the letters of the word ADDRESSING to stand for one of these cultural facets. A is for "age," and in this facet Hays is speaking of the differences that may exist between generations. People who grew up during the Great Depression, for example, may have particular views that govern their thoughts with regard to what should be viewed as a strength or a weakness.[1] The two Ds are for "disability," developmental or acquired. Many of the other facets are more self-explanatory. R is for "religion," E for "ethnicity," S for "socioeconomic status," and S for "sexual orientation." I is for "indigenous heritage" (e.g., American Indian), N is for "nation of origin," and G is for "gender." The idea behind the ADDRESSING framework is that all of these facets may influence the understanding of self and others in the life of any individual.

Certain cultural facets may be more or less salient for any individual, and this is another important part of conceptualization. Only by looking at these facets and evaluating our reactions and sense of belongingness to them can we truly understand cultural identity. Some facets that we do not recognize as salient may still have a prominent place in our lives because of the way we experience them. For example, an individual who has privilege or power as a result of a particular facet (e.g., being a part of the majority race, being male) may not consider this aspect salient in their life, even though it may garner benefits for them day to day. Such individuals may notice that the areas that feel the most salient are the facets in which they do not necessarily enjoy much power or privilege or in which they differ strongly from most people around them. An individual who is from a country other than the United States may find her nation of origin is a very salient feature for her while in the United States. Similarly, an individual who identifies as Muslim may find that his religion is particularly salient to him at his mostly Christian university. Understanding how salience or nonsalience plays a role in using this model to conceptualize one's cultural identity and uncover sources of strength is an important component of this exercise.

Procedure. First, discuss the above material and introduce the ADDRESSING framework. After explaining the major points, ask students to think about which three facets may be most salient for them at their current point in life. Explain that these facets will be discussed in small groups and then in the larger group, so the three facets should be ones that the students are comfortable discussing with others. Once the students have been given time to choose the facets they would like to discuss, direct them to think about the types of positive characteristics they may have cultivated as a result of the facets they have chosen. For example, what positive characteristic might one glean from identifying as a woman, a Catholic, or as an African American? Some facets, such as socioeconomic status, may have multiple factors or groups within them, as well. Thus, different students whose families lie in different strata report different experiences. A student from a lower socioeconomic background may feel that he has cultivated the characteristics of creativity and hope from having to overcome various obstacles in his life. Another student may feel that her higher socioeconomic background has given her more opportunities to cultivate

---

[1]This particular facet is often difficult for students to understand. Many think of "age" in developmental terms, instead of generational terms, and as such might remark that as a young person, age is salient for them because they are the youngest in their work setting. This is not a conceptually correct interpretation of this facet in that having developmental age made salient does not necessarily mean that one's status as a member of a particular generation is made salient at the same time. More examples are often needed here to make sure that students understand this facet correctly.

altruism. Thus, the various cultural facets provide myriad examples that show the diversity of our experiences as cultural beings and as people in general. During this reflection time, students should begin to jot some notes regarding their ideas for discussion with a partner. After 5 minutes or so, students should meet in pairs to discuss their thoughts about these facets and the roles these facets play in developing various positive characteristics. This progression (first self-analysis and then small groups) gives students a chance to collect their thoughts on this topic and primes them to feel more comfortable sharing these experiences and ideas with the larger group. This part of the process can be followed with a more involved group discussion in which students can voluntarily share their thoughts with the entire group.

DISCUSSION

Discussion can begin with the question, "What traits did you identify as coming from your most salient cultural facets?" (Additional discussion questions are offered in the Writing Component section below; these questions can be used as the instructor sees fit and should be guided by the discussion of the students.) The instructor should lead this discussion but encourage students to refer to one another as they make various points about their own cultivated positive characteristics. As students share their thoughts on this topic, similarities and differences between their various ideas might be revealed. Students might also be directed to listen to and "borrow" others' ideas as sources of strength for themselves. Perhaps one student listed being Latino as a source that has caused him to develop strong coping in the face of discrimination, while another, who also listed his Latino heritage, feels he has strong altruistic aims because of the collectivist nature of his background. The two students may benefit from each other's interpretation by broadening their understanding of what this facet can cultivate in their lives. In addition, perhaps a student who identifies strongly with her acquired disability status can relate to the discrimination the first individual discusses and can see how this is a positive trait she may have cultivated from this different facet in Hays's model.

The last part of the discussion can focus on reactions to the characteristics of Hays's model that students did not identify as particularly salient for them. To start this part of the discussion, instructors might ask students to take another look at the ADDRESSING model and note the other facets listed. For example, though many students may remark that they draw specific strength from a religious affiliation, some students may note that they gain strength from lacking affiliation with a particular religion. In their opinion, this might make them more open-minded to all affiliations and help them to cultivate a more multicultural personality as a strength (Ponterotto et al., 2007). Other students might note that being male in a more male-oriented society is not salient for them on a day-to-day basis but that they have cultivated a sense of confidence or self-efficacy as a result of experiencing power and privilege. In today's psychology classrooms, female students may note that they experience the same result in this particular environment due to their often being the majority in these classes. This portion of the discussion is dedicated to fostering multicultural competence in the students as a whole by increasing awareness of privileges that might allow them to use strengths cultivated as a result to assist others who do not have these types of privileges in their lives. In this way, positive psychology may be passed on in a beneficial way to a larger population.

This exercise also has the benefit of pointing out the incredible diversity that exists in any group. Even if a group is fairly homogeneous in terms of race, ethnicity, or socioeconomic status, there are usually enough differences in other facets, or in the ways that students think about these facets, that students can see the wide variety of worldviews that arise from cultural identity. The goal of this exercise is to show how worldview (as a result of cultural identification) can significantly affect the development of (and opportunity to cultivate) various positive characteristics. In addition, it assists in the development of awareness that our own views are biased by our own cultural identity and that we must look beyond these biases to fully understand a characteristic as it "works" or "does not work" in the lives of others.

WRITING COMPONENT

As a writing exercise, students can answer any of the following questions not broached in discussion: (a) How have you cultivated the culturally derived positive characteristic you identified in class? (b) Do you have cultural role models who helped you to recognize this positive characteristic? If so, what did they tell you about it?[2] (c) How do you maintain the use of this trait in everyday life? (d) What positive characteristics might you cultivate from the cultural facets that are not particularly salient for you? (e) How might you cultivate additional positive traits from your various cultural facets after listening to students' reflections from class?[3]

REFERENCES

Hays, P. A. (2008). *Addressing cultural complexities in practice.* Washington, DC: American Psychological Association. doi:10.1037/11650-000

Pedrotti, J. T. (2011). Broadening perspectives: Strategies to infuse multiculturalism into a positive psychology course. *The Journal of Positive Psychology, 6,* 506–513.

Pedrotti, J. T., Edwards, L. M., & Lopez, S. J. (2009). Positive psychology within a cultural context. In S. J. Lopez (Ed.), *Oxford handbook of positive psychology* (pp. 49–57). New York, NY: Oxford University Press.

Ponterotto, J. G., Costa-Wofford, C. I., Brobst, K. E., Spelliscy, D., Kacanski, J. M., Scheinholtz, J., & Martines, D. (2007). Multicultural personality dispositions and psychological well-being. *The Journal of Social Psychology, 147,* 119–135. doi:10.3200/SOCP.147.2.119-135

Snyder, C. R., Lopez, S. J., & Pedrotti, J. T. (2011). *Positive psychology: The scientific and practical explorations of human strengths.* Thousand Oaks, CA: Sage.

---

[2]Remember that "culture" encompasses many facets: A woman might feel that her mother taught her that women are strong relationship builders, for example. In this way, the mother becomes a cultural teacher about what positive characteristics come from being a part of the female gender.
[3]To better grasp this topic, instructors and students are encouraged to consult the following sources: Hays (2008); Pedrotti et al. (2009).

7

PURPOSE
UNDERSTANDING PURPOSE
THROUGH INTERVIEWS
Timothy S. Reilly and William Damon

■──■

The goal of this activity is to bring to life the concept of purpose by illustrating the role that purpose plays in students' own lives. Students are asked to interview each other and then work together to draw a mind map— a diagram that shows the interrelations between the interviewee's values, goals, and actions. The process of creating a mind map illustrates an important way of conceptualizing purpose and provides a foundation for integrating one's purpose into other goals and activities.

■──■

CONCEPT

Purpose during youth is associated with major indicators of thriving during youth and beyond (Bundick, Yeager, King, & Damon, 2010). Therefore, it is a worthwhile goal to make course content on purpose directly relevant to students. Adolescents and young adults often do not have a strong sense of purpose and thus have a difficult time grasping the concept. The activity is meant to ground students' intellectual understanding of purpose by tying it to their own experiences and to the experiences of their peers. It does so by encouraging students to elucidate their own nascent purposes and to help another student to better understand his or her purpose. It also seeks to help students conceptualize purpose as a set of values, goals, and actions that can interact to create a sustained life purpose (Moran, 2009).

MATERIALS NEEDED

The Brief Purpose Interview (Appendix 7.1), a mind map example (Appendix 7.2), and interview technique examples (Appendix 7.3).

INSTRUCTIONS

This activity centers on an interview in which each student elicits from a partner personal life goals and future desired selves, which are ideas about one's desired future that may not be engaged as goals. Because purpose is highly individualized, pair interviews are used in the activity. Any activity that focuses on how someone understands his or her own life and behavior without making comparisons with others—such as a written reflection (see below)—could be appropriate. Interviews are preferred, however, because having an outside observer asking follow-up questions allows interviewees to elaborate on their goals and aspirations in ways that they might not be able to do on their own. The interviews and discussion take at least 30 minutes. If less time is available, a single interview per pair, rather than paired interviews, in which each student interviews the

DOI: 10.1037/14042-008
Activities for Teaching Positive Psychology: A Guide for Instructors, J. J. Froh and A. C. Parks (Editors)
Copyright © 2013 by the American Psychological Association. All rights reserved.

other, should be used. Using the interview serves a number of goals, including increasing students' awareness of the variety of methodologies used in psychological research, as interview research is rare. The interview can also help students to be aware of the highly subjective nature of purpose, both in terms of their own experiences and in terms of their identification of others' purposes.

Ideally, the idea of purpose will have been broached with the class prior to the activity. Purpose is an important aspect of development and provides motivation and direction. It is, however, a difficult concept for many students to grasp. Many young adults do not yet have a fully developed sense of purpose, or, because purpose can manifest in an array of forms, they may have a purpose yet not be consciously aware of it (for examples, see Bronk, 2006; Colby & Damon, 1992; Damon 2008). The term *purpose* is used in research differently from how it is used everyday language. Even within research, there are a variety of definitions of purpose, each with different emphases (e.g., Kashdan & McKnight, 2009; Reker & Wong, 1988; Ryff, 1989). For scientific and educational uses, purpose may be defined in the following manner (see Damon, Menon, & Bronk, 2003):

> A purpose is a stable and generalized intention to accomplish something that is at once meaningful to the self and of consequence to the world beyond the self. A purpose can function as a transcendent goal or "ultimate concern" in life, and thus can organize many other life decisions and actions. A purpose is internalized, or "owned" by the individual, rather than externally driven, and therefore is central to the person's identity.

Purpose is a multidimensional phenomenon; intention, action, plans, and reasons all interact to create a general sense of purpose. Students often find it easier to focus on these more concrete operationalizations—goals, actions, and plans—than on the more abstract concepts of reason or purpose; by identifying goals, actions, and plans, they can indirectly carve a path toward the more abstract question of "why."

Have students form pairs to interview each other, and tell them to switch places after about 10 minutes. In each pair, the interviewer's role is to elicit the interviewee's values and goals and to support the interviewee in elaborating on those goals (see Appendix 7.1). Reasons and means for pursuing those goals should be discussed as fully as possible in the time available, as these are the concepts with which students are likely to struggle the most. It is especially important during the discussion to focus on the interviewee's perspective and experience, not just on the actions that he or she describes. For instance, an interviewee may say that he or she is trying to graduate college, an engagement that likely has a particular meaning for him or her and should be elicited, even if the interviewer thinks he or she understands that meaning. The interviewer should focus on helping the interviewee to discuss his or her values, goals, and actions in a way that others can understand, asking for clarification as often as necessary and avoiding judgment. Interviewees should also be told that they should answer questions only to the extent that they are comfortable, given the privacy concerns and personal nature of the interview.

In addition to taking notes throughout the interview, the interviewer should create a mind map of his or her partner on a separate page. This map is intended to show the interrelations between the interviewee's values, goals, and actions. The connections between these dimensions should be elicited from the interviewee and labeled with reasons, particularly the reasons tying goals and actions to values. Asking "why?" often is encouraged. Checking the mind map with the interviewee and eliciting feedback on it may also be helpful, though interviewers must be careful not to color the interviewee's narrative with their own interpretations; they can and should ask for clarification and elaboration, but they should *not* contribute their own ideas to the discussion or ask leading questions. For example, "Did you feel pressured to go to college by your friends and family?" would be a leading question; a more appropriate question would be, "Did your friends and family play a role in your decision to go to college?" To facilitate the organization of responses given by the interviewee, the interviewer should keep each response separate at first and focus as much possible on obtaining an accurate and unbiased record of the interviewee's responses. As patterns emerge, the interviewer can begin to form clusters of the responses that relate to similar values by marking them with a common symbol such as an asterisk or by listing them together on different parts of the paper. Finally, the interviewer can use this material to begin drawing the mind map.

During the interviews, your role as an instructor is to support students in focusing the interviews on their partner's intentions and to be available to clarify the task. A few clarifications beyond those included in the instructions above are most important: It is appropriate to talk about religion, culture, political, or other sensitive issues if they are relevant, and interviewees are encouraged to talk about all values and goals that are or are not purposeful. In a class of more than 30 students, student groups rather than pairs may be necessary. If this is the case, one student should interview and take notes to guide the interview, another should build the mind map, one should be interviewed, and any additional students should also create mind maps for the interviewee.

Following the interviews, have the interviewees write down what they think their purposes are and have the interviewers write what they think the interviewee's purposes are. In addition, have students compare and contrast their answers. This will serve as the foundation for further discussion, as these interviews often lead individuals to speak about themselves in ways that they do not typically consider in speaking to others. For instance, they may discuss wanting to build more sustainable communities, without having clear answers for how they could do so or without being able to verbalize their reason for that desire. Over the course of these discussions, students sometimes come up with more concrete ways to pursue what might have previously seemed to them an amorphous, unattainable goal; they may even discover that other students share the same goal and similarly had not previously verbalized it.

DISCUSSION

After the interview, using the interviews and any other examples students produce, ask students to consider purpose in a number of ways, beginning with the definition of purpose given above. For instance, discuss with students the role of a purposeful goal as part of a cluster of goals, in which trying to build community coexists with health goals, such as exercise goals, and achievement goals, such as graduation. The focus of this discussion is on how a sense of purpose—derived from one's *existing* goals and activities—can be used to find *new* purposeful goals and activities. As an example, many college students want to give back to the world. This can help to organize educational goals, career goals, and relationship goals, even those that are not part of pursuing the purpose directly, and lead to the selection of a career that allows the kind of purposeful family life they desire. Following this discussion, you might address the engagement of purpose at different points in an individual's life. This should emphasize the different concerns that may exist at different ages and in different settings. For instance, while youths are more likely to be involved in purposeful volunteer activities, they may also be involved in activities that prepare them for future engagement with a purpose (e.g., through education). For adults, engagement with current family- and work-related purposes may be more common. Other dimensions of purpose to discuss include the importance of reasons and meaning in understanding goal pursuit (see Carver & Baird, 1998); for example, how different is it to do community service to help others as opposed to doing community service to build a resume? Similarly, it is worthwhile to explore how and why individuals' purposes are unique and how purpose can support thinking about one's future and about one's place in the world (e.g., how pursuing a purpose may lead an individual to make different life decisions).

Writing Component

If a writing component is desired, it is recommended that you ask students to write about a time in their lives when they felt particularly purposeful in their pursuit of a goal. Ideally, this would take place before the interview activity and help them to reflect on any purposes they might have. The time in students' lives should be extended over months or a year, rather than focusing on a single experience. If they have not had such an experience, ask them to write about an individual who pursues a goal purposefully. Providing students the opportunity to share these responses and continue the discussion after the activity through an online forum or wiki may be valuable as well.

As a potential follow-up or alternative to the interview activity, planning a new way of enacting a purpose can be a useful writing assignment. Ask students to plan how they would spend an hour pursuing a purpose in a way they have not yet experienced and to write a reflection on their purpose and how that experience might inform them about their goals. The instructions for the reflection are as follows:

> Write a one-page reflection on your purpose and anticipated experience. Pay particular attention to what you are attempting to accomplish, how you measure success, how you prepared for the experience, and the likelihood that you would continue pursuing the purpose in this new way.

This assignment could be used to help create or extend a mind map.[1]

References

Bronk, K. C. (2006). *Exemplars of youth purpose: A set of twelve case studies of adolescent commitment.* Unpublished manuscript, Stanford University, Stanford, CA.

Bundick, M., Yeager, D., King, P., & Damon, W. (2010). Thriving across the lifespan. In W. Overton (Ed.), *Handbook of lifespan development* (pp. 882–923). New York, NY: Wiley. doi:10.1002/9780470880166.hlsd001024

Carver, C. S., & Baird, E. (1998). The American Dream revisited: Is it what you want or why you want it that matters? *Psychological Science, 9,* 289–292. doi:10.1111/1467-9280.00057

Colby, A., & Damon, W. (1992). *Some do care: Contemporary lives of moral commitment.* New York, NY: Free Press.

---

[1]To better grasp this topic, instructors and students are encouraged to consult Frankl (1959).

Damon, W. (2008). *The path to purpose.* New York, NY: Free Press.

Damon, W., Menon, J., & Bronk, K. C. (2003). The development of purpose during adolescence. *Applied Developmental Science, 7,* 119–128. doi:10.1207/S1532480 XADS0703_2

Frankl, V. E. (1959). *Man's search for meaning.* Boston, MA: Beacon.

Kashdan, T. B., & McKnight, P. E. (2009). Origins of purpose in life: Refining our understanding of a life well lived. *Psychological Topics, 18,* 303–316.

Moran, S. (2009). Purpose: Giftedness in intrapersonal intelligence. *High Ability Studies, 20,* 143–159. doi:10.1080/13598130903358501

Reker, G. T., & Wong, P. T. P. (1988). Aging as an individual process: Toward a theory of personal meaning. In J. E. Birren & V. L. Bengston (Eds.), *Emergent theories of aging* (pp. 214–246). New York, NY: Springer.

Ryff, C.D. (1989). Happiness is everything or is it? Explorations on the meaning of psychological well-being. *Journal of Personality and Social Psychology, 57*(6).

Appendix 7.1

Brief Purpose Interview[1]

- What is important to you? What do you care about? What matters to you?

- How do you spend your time?

- What do you want to be different about the world?

- What could you do to make the world like that?

- Can you rank the different **values and goals** you have talked about **in order of importance?**

- Why is one value **or goal** more important than others?

Use the following questions for each value **or goal (as identified above):**

- How do you show that (**goal or** value) is important?

- How long has (**goal or** value) been important to you?

- How do you plan on continuing to be involved in (**goal or** value), and for how long?

- How does (**goal or** value) influence your life?

---

[1]Adapted from the Questionnaire From the Youth Purpose Study, pp. 183–186, *The Path to Purpose: How Young People Find Their Calling in Life* by William Damon, 2008, New York, NY: Free Press. Copyright 2008 by William Damon.

Appendix 7.2

Sample Mind Map

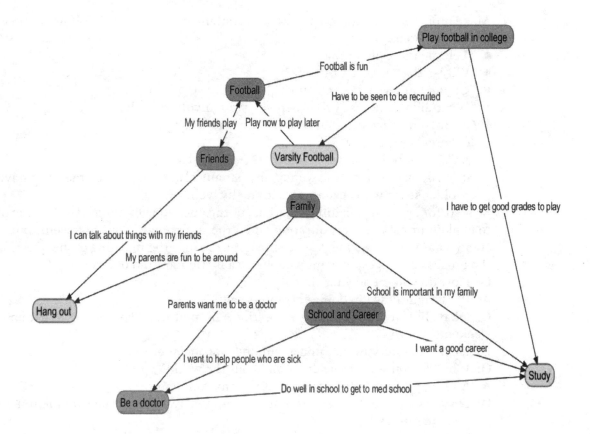

Appendix 7.3

Example Interview Questions

1. Make probes for elaboration as empty of content as possible. The following are good probe questions:
   - "Tell me more about that."
   - "Why is that important to you?"
   - "Could you give me an example?"
   - "What did you actually do when you were involved in that?"
     Q: How long has your family been important to you?
     A: Forever.
     Q: Can you tell me more about that?
     A: Well, even when I was young, my parents always supported me and I have an older sister who I get along with really well.

2. Be alert for apparent misinterpretations of the questions by interviewees. It is okay to explain or paraphrase a question when the interviewee does not seem to understand what you are asking, but be sure not to change the meaning of the question in the process or suggest by your paraphrase a particular kind of answer.
   Q: How do you spend your time?
   A: Well, right now I'm doing this interview.
   Q: Okay, but in general, can you describe a normal weekday for me? What about a weekend?

3. Focus on the interviewee's understanding, not social norms.
   Q: What do you want to be different about the world?
   A: A lot of people really caring about the environment.
   Q: Do you care about the environment, too? Is there a specific environmental cause you are interested in?
   A: When you put it that way, no, I am more interested in helping people than the environment.

4. During the course of the interview, refrain from making evaluative judgments about what the interviewees are saying (e.g., "that's great," "that sounds very cool"). Save your enthusiasm for the end of the interview, when you will be thanking the interviewee for interesting and valuable insights.

8 SPIRITUALITY
SPIRITUAL STRUGGLES AS A FORK IN THE ROAD TO THE SACRED
Maria R. Gear Haugen and Kenneth I. Pargament

The objective of this activity is to broaden and deepen students' knowledge and awareness of spirituality and spiritual struggles by interviewing someone who has experienced adversity and reflecting on this experience through the spiritual lens.

CONCEPT   Life can be conceptualized as a journey that involves all aspects of ourselves as human beings, including the spiritual. We can expect that our spiritual lives will have ups and downs: times of difficulty and challenge as well as times of peace and connectivity to the sacred. Questions, doubts, and conflicts regarding matters of faith, God, and relationships have been termed "spiritual struggles" (Pargament, Murray-Swank, Magyar, & Ano, 2005). These struggles are often believed to be indications of weakness and faithlessness or considered unusual in one's spiritual development. In fact, spiritual struggles are reported by 10% to 65% of Americans (Exline & Rose, 2005). While spiritual struggles are painful to bear, they are a normal part of spiritual development and reflect a spiritual framework that is "straining at the seams."

One's response to spiritual struggles can lead to spiritual development and growth or to significant problems and spiritual stagnation. Anticipating, understanding, and addressing spiritual struggles may help encourage those facing these forks in the road to follow a path of spiritual progress and transformation (Pargament, 2007).

To promote spiritual development, it is important to understand how aspects of one's spirituality may ameliorate the suffering that accompanies spiritual struggles. From a broader perspective, we can assist people at risk for spiritual struggles in several ways: Identify those struggling with their spirituality, create accepting forums in which to discuss spiritual difficulties, and provide guidance and support; normalize spiritual struggles; and anticipate spiritual difficulties as a way to inoculate against future challenges. These helping activities must rest on a reformulation of spiritual development—an acknowledgment that times of darkness and drought are potentially fruitful and grace-filled—and on community-building efforts to provide those experiencing spiritual struggles with the comfort, consolation, and succor they so desperately need.

DOI: 10.1037/14042-009
Activities for Teaching Positive Psychology: A Guide for Instructors, J. J. Froh and A. C. Parks (Editors)

Recording device of some kind: electronic, computer, or paper and pen; sample interview questions (see Appendix 8.1).

This assignment involves interviewing someone who has experienced a difficulty in his or her life, reflecting on this interview in terms of Pargament, Murray-Swank, Magyar, and Ano's (2005) framework of spiritual struggles, and then writing it up. As the first part of this assignment, students will hand in their "prospectus," which should specify their organization of the items that will be covered in the interview, how they will record the interview(s), and their script for approaching these sensitive topics with the interviewee. Tell the students that their interviews should include basic information about the event and focus on three discrete areas of spiritual struggle (i.e., with the divine, with others, and within the person). Students could use the sample interview questions in Appendix 8.1 and take notes separately.

Tell students to bring the completed assignment to class. Have them break out into small groups of three to five to discuss the assignment. Because this can be a sensitive topic, it is important to establish ground rules for the class before the start of this activity. Ground rules include respecting diversity of opinions and confidentiality as it relates to interviewee identities. The discussion should start with a brief, anonymous account of each interviewee's adversity and the ways in which the experience affected the interviewee spiritually. Further discussion should incorporate the students' reflections on their own understanding of spiritual struggles. Specific topics to include for student discussion include the following:

- Has this exercise affected your acceptance of spiritual struggles as a normal part of spiritual development?
- Has this activity caused you to articulate and explore your own spiritual struggles?
- In what way(s) has this assignment caused you to think differently about adversity as it relates to the spiritual journey?
- How do you believe this exercise will affect the way you deal with adversity in your life?

Relevance of Spiritual Struggles to Students: Emerging adulthood, the period of transition from adolescence to adulthood, is commonly a time of personal development in which existential or spiritual questions may rise to the fore. In their study of religious and spiritual concerns among a national sample of college students, Johnson and Hayes (2003) found that 26% of students reported "considerable distress" resulting from religious and spiritual problems, and one third of students who receive services at university counseling centers reported at least some level of such distress. Early emerging adulthood (i.e., to age 20) is also a time of increased exposure to traumatic and adverse life events. Exploration of these issues can lead to spiritual confusion and doubts as well as psychological and spiritual distress, although this is not inevitable. Given the prevalence of spiritual struggles and trauma exposure for this population, anticipating, understanding, and addressing spiritual challenges are of particular relevance and significance.

Spiritual Struggles Within a Stress and Coping Framework: What determines whether spiritual struggles lead to growth or decline? Although empirical research in this area is scant, it is plausible that the religious and spiritual coping framework parallels, at least in part, attributes of secular coping. Lazarus and Folkman's (1984) model of stress and coping indicates that the individual's worldview, including assumptions, beliefs, values, and resources, influences responses to stress. In a similar vein, Pargament, Desai, and McConnell (2006) defined the spiritual orienting system (SOS) as "contributing to the individual's framework for understanding and dealing with the world" (p. 130). These authors identified four factors as key to the development of a resilient SOS: spiritual integration, flexibility, differentiation, and benevolence.

Spiritual integration reflects the degree to which religious and spiritual beliefs and practices are congruent with one another and permeate one's daily life. Empirical studies indicate that higher levels of spiritual integration are associated with higher levels of physical and psychological health.

Although spiritual integration refers to consistency across spiritual beliefs and practices, *spiritual flexibility* is the amount of plasticity in one's religiousness or spirituality, particularly in response to unexpected events. Spiritual flexibility does not intimate a relativistic or weak-willed position, but rather the capacity to respond to a given situation, person, or event in more than one way and in accordance with the demands of precipitating circumstances. Those with rigid spiritual worldviews may have difficulty in adjusting to life's challenges and potentially leads to spiritual strain.

Spiritual differentiation is that aspect of the SOS that allows for an appreciation of the paradox, mystery, and complexity of religion and spirituality while avoiding the tendency to oversimplify situations, events, or ideas. It comes into play when we are faced with situations that are outside of our frame of reference or defy our understanding of ourselves, the world, and others, and it enables us to remain engaged despite that incomprehensibility. Those with a high degree of spiritual differentiation are able, in these situations, to tolerate their discomfort and seek a deeper understanding.

Finally, an individual's SOS can be characterized by its degree of *benevolence.* This may encompass one's image of the divine and experience of religious or spiritual community. Feeling comfort, solace, support, and protection in relationship with the divine can be more effective in resolving spiritual struggles than feeling alienation, anger, insecurity, fear, and disappointment with the divine. Likewise, communities that allow open discussion of spiritual struggles within a context of empathy, caring, and support, rather than shame, guilt, and judgment, will facilitate more positive outcomes.

DISCUSSION

Spirituality, particularly spiritual difficulties, questions, and doubts, can be difficult to articulate and painful to recount. For this reason, it is important to prepare students undertaking this assignment to establish trust and sensitivity to the interviewee; exercise tolerance of differing belief systems; and be ready with specific, thought-provoking questions and topics for the interviews. The first part of the assignment, the prospectus, was designed to facilitate the instructor's review of these points and to provide feedback to students before the interviews.

Immediately before the breakout session for small-group discussion, instructors should remind students of the ground rules as they apply to this situation. Instructors should also reiterate the basic points of this activity: Spiritual struggles are a normal part of life; exploration of issues related to spiritual struggles within a supportive (not judgmental) environment contributes to positive outcomes; what to do if this activity leads to feeling of distress or discomfort.

After students have completed the interview and read Pargament's delineation of spiritual struggles (Pargament et al., 2006), they should be instructed to reflect on their interviewee's experience in terms of this framework. Their writeup should include details about the interview and how this person's experience fits into Pargament's framework. Their view of what impact(s) this experience has had on their understanding of adversity and spiritual development should be included.[1]

REFERENCES

Exline, J. J., & Rose, E. (2005). Religious and spiritual struggles. In R. F. Paloutizian & C. L. Park (Eds.), *Handbook of the psychology of religion and spirituality* (pp. 315–330). New York, NY: Guilford Press.

Johnson, C. V., & Hayes, J. A. (2003). Troubled spirits: Prevalence and predictors of religious and spiritual concerns among university students and counseling center clients. *Journal of Counseling Psychology, 50,* 409–419. doi:10.1037/0022-0167.50.4.409

Lazarus, R. S., & Folkman, S. (1984). *Stress, appraisal, and coping.* New York, NY: Springer.

Pargament, K. I. (2007). Times of stress: Spiritual coping to transform the sacred. In *Spiritually integrated psychotherapy* (pp. 111–128). New York, NY: Guilford Press.

Pargament, K. I., Desai, K. M., & McConnell, K. M. (2006). Spirituality: A pathway to posttraumatic growth or decline? In L. G. Calhoun & R. G. Tedeschi (Eds.), *Handbook of posttraumatic growth: Research and practice* (pp. 121–137). Mahwah, NJ: Erlbaum.

Pargament, K. I., Murray-Swank, N., Magyar, G., & Ano, G. (2005). Spiritual struggle: A phenomenon of interest to psychology and religion. In W. R. Miller & H. Delaney (Eds.), *Judeo-Christian perspectives on psychology: Human nature, motivation, and change* (pp. 245–268). Washington DC: American Psychological Association.

---

[1]To better grasp this topic, instructors and students are encouraged to consult the following sources: Exline and Rose (2005); Pargament (2007); Pargament et al. (2005, 2006).

Appendix 8.1

Interview guide: Explain the assignment to your interviewee. Ask for their permission to talk in detail about an adversity in their life before you begin. Assure them of confidentiality. If it is helpful to you, place a check in the box next to each question after you ask about it.

Background information:

What is important for me to know in order to understand this situation? ☐

Were there any aspects of the sacred or of a spiritual nature to the event? ☐

Would you say this event has affected you spiritually? ☐ How so? ☐

Spiritual struggles—broken out into the three types:

With the divine—Ask what term your interviewee uses for the transcendent, for example, God, higher power, the sacred, and then use this term throughout the interview.

Did you perceive the event as a sacred loss or a violation of something sacred to you? ☐

Were you angry at God (the sacred or your higher power)? ☐

Did you have difficulty understanding how the transcendent could allow this to occur? ☐

Did this event change your perception of the divine? If so, in what way, specifically? ☐

With others:

Did you blame someone for this event? ☐ If so, have you been able to forgive? ☐

How did this relationship change as a result of this event? ☐

How did this event affect your religious practices, for example, prayer, worship, or other activities? ☐

Within the person (intrapsychic):

Did you experience a spiritual conflict, questions, or doubts about matters of faith? ☐

Did you blame yourself for any part of this event? If so, what did you do with this guilt? ☐

Did your values or priorities or the way you view life your life change? ☐

II
EXPERIMENTS

PURPOSE

Activities in this part involve experimental manipulations of the target concept, with students as the "participants"; instructors can then use aggregated data from the class and the anecdotal experiences of the students to illustrate the concept. These activities give students firsthand experience with the research methods they are learning about in class or in their reading, bringing them to life in a way that makes the content more engaging and personally relevant.

OVERVIEW OF ACTIVITIES

Bethany E. Kok and Barbara Fredrickson contribute a chapter on **Positive Emotion** in which they illustrate the impact of emotion on creativity; mirroring lab studies on positive emotion, students engage in a problem-solving task after receiving either a positive or a neutral mood induction, and the instructor compares task performance across the two groups. Sarah D. Pressman and Tara L. Kraft focus on the ability of positive emotional experiences to affect one's physiology in **Positive Health**; students undergo mood inductions and record the effects of these experiences on their heart rate. Shelly L. Gable, in her chapter on **Relationships**, contributes an in-class demonstration of a positive process that is predictive of relationship longevity and satisfaction: responding actively and constructively to good news from other people. Students are split into pairs, and in each pair, one student shares a positive event while the other student is randomly assigned to respond in one of several possible ways. In the chapter by Michael W. Myers and Sara D. Hodges, students learn about **Empathy** by reading a vignette about a person in need and rating their feelings toward that person after receiving one of two prompts: one that promotes empathy and one that promotes psychological distance. In their chapter about the relationship between **Culture and Subjective Well-Being**, Christie Napa Scollon, Derrick Wirtz, and Xuan-yi Wei prime students with either an "individualistic" or a "collectivistic" mind-set, then compare between-group responses to well-being survey items. Lara B. Aknin and Elizabeth W. Dunn illustrate the relationship between **Wealth and Subjective Well-Being** with an activity in which students rate their happiness after recalling in detail either a time they spent money on themselves or a time they spent money on someone else. Shauna L. Shapiro and Timothy R. Mariels ask students to observe and reflect on their experiences while engaging in neutral, pleasant, and anxiety-provoking activities using the principles of **Mindfulness**. Everett Worthington, Aubrey L. Gartner, David J. Jennings II, and Don E. Davis contribute an activity in which students observe, participate in, and subsequently learn to lead a manualized group intervention designed to promote **Forgiveness**. David J. Shernoff and Brett Anderson provide a tool for measuring **Flow** among students in the classroom and guidelines for systematically manipulating their experience of flow. Students gain firsthand experience with flow as a process, as well as the research methodology (experience sampling) that is often used to study flow states.

9 POSITIVE EMOTION
HOW POSITIVE EMOTIONS BROADEN
AND BUILD

Bethany E. Kok and Barbara L. Fredrickson

This activity allows students to reenact a classic social psychological experiment on the cognitive effects of positive emotions. Students attempt to solve a puzzle that requires flexible, creative thinking while experiencing either neutral or positive emotions, then discuss how their emotions influenced their problem-solving strategies.

CONCEPT

The broaden-and-build theory of positive emotions (Fredrickson, 1998, 2003) posits that positive emotions are distinct from negative emotions and have different effects over the short and long terms. Over the short term, positive emotions widen the repertoire of peoples' possible actions, resulting in creativity. Positive emotions also widen the attentional scope, causing people to notice more of their environment and to pay more attention to what is going on around them. Positive emotions also create openness to new experiences. In contrast, negative emotions cause people to narrow their focus and reject new experiences in favor of the safe and familiar. Essentially, while negative emotions narrow a person's repertoire of thoughts, actions, and interests, positive emotions broaden it. In the long term, multiple moments of broadening add up to create resources, such as physical health, new skills, new knowledge, and better relationships, that can help people during hard times.

The purpose of this activity is to reenact an early classic study on positive emotions and cognition by Isen, Daubman, and Nowicki (1987). In this study, students whose positive emotions were increased through the gift of a small bag of candy showed greater problem-solving ability in a subsequent task. Isen et al. interpreted this as evidence that positive emotions increase creativity. The activity demonstrates three concepts: (a) random assignment to conditions (positive emotion condition versus neutral condition), (b) inducing positive emotions in the laboratory, and (c) the effect of positive emotions on creativity.

MATERIALS NEEDED

Calculator to compute percentages.

Positive Emotion Induction: One small bag of candy (Isen et al., 1987, used three or four candies wrapped in clear plastic and tied with a ribbon) for each student in the positive emotion condition (50% of the class). It is nice to give the remaining students the bags of candy at the end of the activity.

DOI: 10.1037/14042-010
Activities for Teaching Positive Psychology: A Guide for Instructors, J. J. Froh and A. C. Parks (Editors)

Problem-Solving Task—Duncker Candle Task (Duncker, 1945): Per student: One tea candle or other small candle, one box of matches, and one thumbtack. Per class: One corkboard attached to a wall in the back of the classroom.

INSTRUCTIONS

Randomly assign students to either the experimental or the control condition by flipping a coin, using an online number generator, or any other method of your choice. Ask students in the control condition to wait in the hallway. Give each student in the experimental condition a bag of candy. Make sure to ask them to put the bags away so that the students in the control condition cannot see them, then let the students in the control condition back in. This is to make sure that students in the control condition are experiencing neutral emotions, rather than negative ones such as jealousy or disappointment that they do not get candy. Students should also not eat any candy until after the study is complete to make sure any effects are due to emotional causes rather than increased blood glucose levels.

Next, hand out the Duncker candle task materials to each student, and read them the following instructions:

> Your goal is to attach the candle to the corkboard in such a way that it will burn without dripping wax onto the table or the floor beneath it. You can use only the materials you have been given. When you think you have a solution, please bring your materials to the corkboard to demonstrate it. Please do not talk among yourselves. You have 3 minutes.

Stand by the corkboard, which should, if possible, be placed in the back of the classroom so that students cannot see one another's solutions. Have students approach you one at a time and demonstrate how they have solved the problem. After each demonstration, remove the student's materials so the board is clear for the next student. Students who give an incorrect solution should be allowed to go back to their desk and continue trying to solve the puzzle. At the end of the 3-minute period, ask all students to stop. Count how many students in each condition (experimental vs. control) successfully solved the problem, and write the percentages on the board for discussion.

If you are concerned that some students may become bored while waiting for others to solve the task, you can assign them to read part or all of an introductory chapter on the broaden-and-build theory by Kok, Catalino, and Fredrickson (2008).

Candle Task Solution: Take the tray out of the matchbox and attach it to the corkboard with the thumbtack, thus forming a shelf on which to set the candle.

DISCUSSION

The Duncker candle task measures problem-solving ability, an important survival trait in the evolutionary past and in the present. The task presents a problem that cannot be solved through linear, connect-the-dot reasoning. The problem can be solved, however, through the use of holistic, "outside-the-box" thinking—the kind of thinking that positive emotions encourage.

According to the broaden-and-build theory of positive emotions (Fredrickson, 1998, 2001, 2003), positive emotions have long-term psychological effects as a result of the buildup of benefits from many short-term experiences of broadening, experiences such as the creative thinking required to solve the Duncker candle task. Short-term increases in creativity, problem-solving ability, attentional scope, and openness to experience lead to making healthier, wiser life choices, which have the effect of building a person's social, psychological, intellectual, and physical resources. This increase in resources is demonstrated by better coping in adversity, increased relationship closeness, mindfulness, and improved immune functioning.

Positive emotions leading to increased resources, in turn leading to more positive emotions, is an example of "upward spiral." The result of this spiral is a bank of long-term resources that increase resilience in the face of trouble and make life richer and more meaningful.

Suggested topics for discussion include the following: (a) Did the experiment work? If not, have students brainstorm why the experiment failed. Possible reasons include the positive emotion induction not being effective, the problem-solving task being too hard or too easy or not actually assessing creativity, or random assignment somehow being ineffective. What makes an experiment good or bad? (b) Assuming the experiment worked, ask the students what they think of a candy gift as a way of increasing positive emotions. Note that Isen et al. (1987) also used other induction methods, such as leaving change in public phone booths for others to find and watching humorous videos. Discuss the pros and cons of each. (c) How might experiencing moments of creativity like this lead to building resources and long-term positive consequences?

WRITING COMPONENT Ask students to introspect on their internal thought processes as they tried to solve the problem. How they felt (hopeful, curious, irritated, frustrated), what was going through their mind (focused on the problem, distracted), how they think they discovered the solution. Students can also write about a time in their lives when they were faced with a similar problem and whether they think their emotions played a role in solving it.[1]

REFERENCES Duncker, K. (1945). On problem solving. *Psychological Monographs, 58,* i–113. doi:10.1037/h0093599

Fredrickson, B. L. (1998). What good are positive emotions? *Review of General Psychology, 2,* 300–319. doi:10.1037/1089-2680.2.3.300

Fredrickson, B. L. (2001). The role of positive emotions in positive psychology: The broaden-and-build theory of positive emotions. *American Psychologist, 56,* 218–226. doi:10.1037/0003-066X.56.3.218

Fredrickson, B. L. (2003). The value of positive emotions. *American Scientist, 91,* 330–335.

Fredrickson, B. L., & Branigan, C. (2003). Positive emotions broaden the scope of attention and thought-action repertoires. *Cognition and Emotion, 19,* 313–332. doi:10.1080/02699930441000238

Fredrickson, B. L., Cohn, M. A., Coffey, K. A., Pek, J., & Finkel, S. M. (2008). Open hearts build lives: Positive emotions, induced through loving-kindness meditation, build consequential personal resources. *Journal of Personality and Social Psychology, 95,* 1045–1062. doi:10.1037/a0013262

Isen, A. M., Daubman, K. A., & Nowicki, G. P. (1987). Positive affect facilitates creative problem solving. *Journal of Personality and Social Psychology, 52,* 1122–1131. doi:10.1037/0022-3514.52.6.1122

Kok, B. E., Catalino, L. I., & Fredrickson, B. L. (2008). The broadening, building, buffering effects of positive emotions. In S. J. Lopez (Ed.), *Positive psychology: Exploring the best of people: Vol. 3 Capitalizing on emotional experiences.* (pp. 1–19). Westport, CT: Greenwood Press.

---

[1]To better grasp this topic, instructors and students are encouraged to consult the following sources: Fredrickson (1998); Fredrickson and Branigan (2003); Fredrickson, Cohn, Coffey, Pek, and Finkel (2008); Isen et al. (1987); Kok et al. (2008).

10

POSITIVE HEALTH
HEART RATE VARIATION WITH POSITIVE PSYCHOLOGY EXERCISES

Sarah D. Pressman and Tara L. Kraft

This activity allows students who have discussed the health implications of positive psychology to see an example of how positive psychology exercises affect their own physiology and provides an opportunity to discuss the meaning of these changes. Over a short (approximately 15-minute) period, students will record their resting heart rate and their heart rate in response to two positive mood-inducing activities.

CONCEPT

Heart rate (HR) is an important measure for in diagnosing medical conditions. This is typically done by using an electrocardiograph; however, the pulse of the heart can also be felt by simply holding your fingers over an artery. Resting HR is typically 60 to 100 beats per minute (bpm), with low HR (below 50 bpm) or high HR (above 100 bpm) sometimes indicating health problems (e.g., heart disease, hormone issues) or health behaviors like smoking, stimulant consumption, or drug use. Low HR is considered normal if the individual has no negative symptoms and is often found in athletes.

HR varies with the body's metabolic needs. For example, during exercise, HR increases greatly because of the increased need for oxygen and blood in the muscles. The heart responds similarly to psychological stress and other negative emotions despite the lack of increased metabolic need. (You do not need the same types of muscle activity when sitting at your desk studying for a hard exam!) More recently, researchers have also noted that positive feelings can have a beneficial impact on the heart. Specifically, some positive states result in decreased HRs that may be beneficial, particularly when heart activity has been heightened as a result of stress. Some arousing or activated positive states, such as laughter, may increase HR in the short term. This is typically thought to be more similar to exercise, with increases being brief when compared with negative states, which produce long-lasting HR increases, and possibly chronic elevations, due to dysregulated heart function and rumination.

This exercise allows students to note their own cardiovascular changes produced via positive psychology exercises. We recommend picking two exercises: one low-arousal activity (e.g., mindfulness) and one high-arousal activity (e.g., watching a comedy). Please refer to Appendix 10.1 for Web resources (the URLs were up to date at the publication of this book, but if they do not function, please try using a search engine to

---

DOI: 10.1037/14042-011

Activities for Teaching Positive Psychology: A Guide for Instructors, J. J. Froh and A. C. Parks (Editors)
Copyright © 2013 by the American Psychological Association. All rights reserved.

track down these or similar exercises). Students will record their resting HR and their HR immediately on completion of each of the exercises.

A timing device (e.g., a stopwatch) is needed to record the time period for HR measurement. If HR monitors or applications on cellular phones can be used if they are available, but they are not necessary. A computer and projector with sound capability are suggested to show the video.

In choosing an exercise, use what you think will be most applicable to your class based on what you have been teaching. Keep the following in mind in selecting the exercise instructions or video. Many of the instructional videos we found were poor in quality, distracting, or not well done. Be sure to evaluate quality before using one in class. You should also try to focus on an exercise that will be engaging without requiring a lot of movement. It is compelling for students to see the simple impact of the power of the mind over their heart function, even when they are sitting still.

INSTRUCTIONS

Read the following statement to your students:

> To gather data on how different psychological variables influence heart rate, you will record your heart rate at several time points: before participating in any of the exercises (a baseline assessment) and immediately after engaging in various positive psychology activities.

We recommend that you instruct your students to feel their pulses with their middle and index fingers either on the underside (ventral side) of the wrist or on the side of the neck just below the jaw (carotid artery) because these two points are easy to use in a classroom setting. Showing a picture of the preferred pulse locations to the group (freely available online or in medical texts) is helpful at this point. The thumb should not be used because of its strong pulse. Instruct students to be silent and keep still to accurately count how many times they feel their pulse beat in a 15-second increment. Once this number is obtained, instruct them to multiply that number by 4 to obtain the total bpms. Resting HR should be 60 to 80 bpm. Once a baseline measurement has been taken, proceed to complete two positive psychology exercises so that the students can examine the resulting changes in bpm.

For the second measurement, you will guide the students through a relaxing/calming positive exercise for 2 to 3 minutes. We recommend mindfulness, guided positive imagery, loving-kindness meditation, or a form of guided gratitude. Because students' minds may wander (making the activity less effective), we recommend using either a video or reading the instructions as they do the exercise and dimming the lights to improve adherence and engagement. Instructions will vary depending on the exercise chosen. For example, a typical set of verbal instructions for a mindfulness exercise might include reminding the class to focus on their breathing or to direct their attention to various body sensations (e.g., asking them to become mindful of their feet against the floor, their posture, or how clothing feels as it touches their skin).

Once the exercise is complete, quietly instruct the students to begin a second HR measurement for 15 seconds. Have the students mark down their response and multiply it by 4 for their second "calming positive" bpm.

For the active positive exercise, read the following statement to your students: "I will play a video shortly. Please watch the following video and record your heart rate

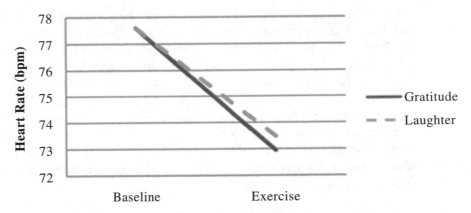

Figure 10.1. *The impact of positive psychology exercises on heart rate. Heart rate changes following two types of positive psychology exercises in an undergraduate class at a large Midwestern university (N = 90).*

when it is complete." For our class, we used a 2-minute laughter yoga instructional video; however, multiple studies have shown that positive movies and comedic clips also affect heart function (e.g., Harrison et al., 2000; Uchiyama et al., 1990; Waldstein et al., 2000). After the clip, begin a second HR measurement for 15 seconds. Have the students mark down their response and multiply it by 4 for their second "active positive" bpm. Once the activity has been completed, poll the class for their results (e.g., How many observed a decrease in HR from baseline following the exercises? How many saw an increase?) and begin discussion. We recommend collecting student results and graphing the class average as discussed below. You might also have students volunteer to graph their findings on the board for observation of a few data points and to demonstrate individual variability in activity effectiveness.

DISCUSSION

In our experience, a **decrease in HR** that is similar across different types of activities generally follows the positive exercises (Figure 10.1). Discussion should focus on the fact that a lower HR can be beneficial for health and can be especially helpful in times of stress to alleviate negative arousal. This is compatible with the idea that positive emotions can "undo" the stress response (i.e., Fredrickson, Mancuso, Branigan, & Tugade, 2000). Calling on a positive psychology exercise when feeling negative has an impact not only on psychological well-being but also on physical well-being, as has been demonstrated by the HR changes following the activities.

Some students will report more difficulty with this exercise than others. In our class, for example, some had a hard time concentrating on the exercises for an extended period without their minds wandering. This may result in different HR trends for some individuals. It is helpful to explain to students that, given the known individual differences in positive psychology exercise effectiveness for happiness outcomes, differences in physiological effectiveness are not surprising. This can lead to a discussion of finding a "fit" for positive psychology exercises in general and how some exercises will not be a good match for some individuals.

Some students may be surprised that the active exercise (laughing) resulted in a posttest decrease in HR. Explain the difference between what is likely to occur during versus after the laughter. Although laughing is arousing, albeit to a lesser extent than physical activity, the critical element is that the measurement occurs when the body is relaxing after the arousing state. Thus, despite the counterintuitive finding that active positivity increases HR during the activity, the benefit is in the aftereffects. Note: If the class has access to an automated HR monitor, students will be able to examine the HR increase and decrease more precisely, although doing this by hand is not recommended since it will prevent engagement with the mood manipulations.

Students should be urged to try this exercise at home with various types of positive activities that have been discussed in class to find the ones that result in the greatest physiological benefits for them. They should also be encouraged to try this exercise during a stressful period to see the beneficial impact it can have on relaxing their cardiovascular system.

WRITING COMPONENT

1. Were you able to fully participate and engage in the exercises? Why or why not? How do you think your participation affected your HR? Do you think that one exercise was more effective in lowering your HR? Why?
2. How do you think doing one of these exercises would affect your heart function during times of stress?
3. What are the health implications of these positive psychology exercises? Describe the mechanisms that might explain these health outcomes.
4. Can you think of a different positive psychology activity that might be even more effective for lowering your HR?[1]

REFERENCES

Clark, A., Seidler, A., & Miller, M. (2001). Inverse association between sense of humor and coronary heart disease. *International Journal of Cardiology, 80,* 87–88. doi:10.1016/S0167-5273(01)00470-3

Fredrickson, B. L., & Levenson, R. W. (1998). Positive emotions speed recovery from the cardiovascular sequelae of negative emotions. *Cognition and Emotion, 12,* 191–220. doi:10.1080/026999398379718

Fredrickson, B. L., Mancuso, R. A., Branigan, C., & Tugade, M. M. (2000). The undoing effect of positive emotions. *Motivation and Emotion, 24,* 237–258. doi:10.1023/A:1010796329158

Harrison, L. K., Carroll, D., Burns, V. E., Corkill, A. R., Harrison, C. M., Ring, C., & Drayson, M. (2000). Cardiovascular and secretory immunoglobulin A reactions to humorous, exciting, and didactic film presentations. *Biological Psychology, 52,* 113–126. doi:10.1016/S0301-0511(99)00033-2

Kubzansky, L. D., & Thurston, R. C. (2007). Emotional vitality and incident coronary heart disease: Benefits of healthy psychological functioning. *Archives of General Psychiatry, 64,* 1393–1401. doi:10.1001/archpsyc.64.12.1393

Miller, M., & Fry, W. F. (2009). The effect of mirthful laughter on the human cardiovascular system. *Medical Hypotheses, 73,* 636–639. doi:10.1016/j.mehy.2009.02.044

---

[1]To better grasp this topic, instructors and students are encouraged to consult the following sources: Clark, Seidler, and Miller (2009); Fredrickson and Levenson (1998); Kubzansky and Thurston (2007); Miller and Fry (2009); Pressman and Cohen (2005).

Pressman, S. D., & Cohen, S. (2005). Does positive affect influence health? *Psychological Bulletin, 131*, 925–971. doi:10.1037/0033-2909.131.6.925

Uchiyama, I., Hanari, T., Ito, T., Takahashi, K., Okuda, T., Goto, T., & Keiichiro, T. (1990). Patterns of psychological and physiological responses for common affects elicited by films. *Psychologia. An International Journal of Psychology in the Orient, 33*(1), 36–41.

Waldstein, S. R., Kop, W. J., Schmidt, L. A., Haufler, A. J., Krantz, D. S., & Fox, N. A. (2000). Frontal electrocortical and cardiovascular reactivity during happiness and anger. *Biological Psychology, 55*, 3–23. doi:10.1016/S0301-0511(00)00065-X

Appendix 10.1

LAUGHTER MATERIALS

Laughter Yoga DVDs, manuals, and instructional videos can be found here: http://www.laughteryoga.org/Many brief videos are available at YouTube (http://www.youtube.com) and can be accessed by searching on "laughter exercise." Two examples that we used can be found at http://www.youtube.com/watch?v=Y1raCV_jfPQ and http://www.youtube.com/watch?v=k9iOxL4C0u8 (the latter requires a classroom large enough for movement). In the emotions literature, it is common to use stand-up comedy clips from icons such as Bill Cosby, Robin Williams, or Jerry Seinfeld to induce laughter. Such clips might be useful for this exercise, although again, please consider your population when picking the clip to ensure broad appeal.

GRATITUDE OR LOVING-KINDNESS MATERIALS

Audio gratitude exercise instructions from Deepak Chopra were used for our calming positive exercise. An example of this type of exercise can be found at http://www.youtube.com/watch?v=TIXIwdhOmSM, although there are many similar alternatives. Ideally, pick an activity that matches with past class discussions or exercises. Many alternative mindfulness exercises that would be appropriate for this activity are available on YouTube, at other locations, and for purchase. Loving-kindness meditations tend to be longer than the allotted 2- to 3-minute period; however, if your class time allows, you will see cardiovascular alterations with longer clips (e.g., audio CD exercises by Sharon Salzberg).

11 RELATIONSHIPS
CAPITALIZING ON POSITIVE EVENTS
Shelly L. Gable

This in-class experimental demonstration assists students in understanding the four different types of responses to positive event disclosures.

CONCEPT

This activity introduces students to the concept of capitalization interactions, in which one person talks about something positive that happened to him or her and another person responds to that disclosure. Students are often more familiar with the concept of traditional social support, in which one person talks about something bad or stress in his or her life and the other person responds to that disclosure.

MATERIALS NEEDED

Students will receive different instructions based on the condition and role to which they are randomly assigned. These instructions will need to be prepared in advance in accordance with the number of students participating in the exercise.

INSTRUCTIONS

This activity should take place before students have discussed the concept of capitalizing on positive events. Ideally, this exercise should immediately precede the class lecture on the topic.

1. Divide the students into two equal groups: *interviewers* and *interviewees*. If the number of students is odd, put the extra person in the interviewee group.
2. Give each interviewee a copy of the following instructions:

   > Today you will be interviewed by a fellow student about something good that happened to you. It does not matter what type of event you choose to talk about or how important that event is or was, as long as you are comfortable talking about it and it was a positive event or thing that happened. The event can be something that happened last week or something that happened as long as 1 year ago. It can be any type of event that you are comfortable talking about. The person interviewing you will ask you to describe the event and then may or may not choose to follow up with additional questions. During the interview try to remember how you feel while you are talking about this event and how you feel about the nature of your interaction with the interviewer.

3. Give each interviewer one of four different types of instructions. This will serve as a random assignment. Do not draw attention to the fact that there are different instructions; most important, the interviewees should not be aware of this.

DOI: 10.1037/14042-012

Activities for Teaching Positive Psychology: A Guide for Instructors, J. J. Froh and A. C. Parks (Editors)
Copyright © 2013 by the American Psychological Association. All rights reserved.

An efficient way to do this is to have the instructions printed up and randomly ordered in a pile and then hand one sheet to each interviewer. The four different instructions all begin with "Please ask the person whom you are assigned to interview to describe his or her positive event. Do not show him or her instructions." From this point they differ as follows:

- Active–constructive (AC) responses to people's good events convey interest and enthusiasm regarding the event and positive regard toward the person. These responses often entail questions about the event, elaboration of the positive features, and comments on the implications the event has for a person. The AC responder is often enthusiastic, excited, or happy. To convey this during your interview, make good eye contact, show positive emotion, make enthusiastic comments, such as "That sounds great" or "You must be (have been) so excited." Ask constructive questions to get at more positive aspects of the event (e.g., if a student tells you about a good grade she received on a particularly difficult assignment or test, you might ask questions about how she managed to study or work for the assignment, what aspect she feels really good about, and how this grade will help her in the class or her overall academic plans). Comment on the potential benefits or implications that may come (or have come) from this event. You may take some notes on the event. In short, try to be an active and supportive interviewer. Many people, when they first hear about this style, worry that when they try to do it, especially with people they do not know very well, their responses will sound phony or scripted. However, in practice, once they start, people report it being easy to do. One strategy is to pick one aspect of the event or how the person feels about the event that resonates with you and begin by commenting on that—"I can see that you are happy about that, please tell me more" or "It must have been so satisfying to do so well on something you worked so hard for."

- Passive–constructive (PC) responses may appear positive or supportive on the surface, but they are reserved and subtle. These responses are often quiet exchanges that involve few, if any, questions about the event and little or no elaboration on the implications of the positive event. To convey this during your interview, smile and make occasional eye contact as your interviewee tells you about the event. You may take some notes, but do not ask additional questions about the event or elaborate on his or her statements. When the interviewee is finished speaking, ask whether he or she is done, smile warmly, and say, "That sounds good." In short, try to be a pleasant but uninvolved interviewer.

- Passive–destructive (PD) responses are those in which the responder shows little or no interest in the positive event. The responder may change the subject completely or talk instead about himself or herself. To convey this during the interview, allow the person to talk about the event until he or she has finished the description. Try not to make much eye contact or look too interested in what the interviewee is saying. You may take some notes on the event. When he or she is done, do not comment on the event, but instead continue the conversation in another direction. You can talk about yourself or you can ask him or her mundane questions about everyday life (e.g., "What did you have for breakfast?"). The important part of this interview, once he or she has finished describing the event, is to not contaminate his or her experience by commenting on it or acknowledging the event or emotions surrounding it. Your job is to be a detached and uninterested interviewer.

- Active–destructive (AD) responses are those in which the responder is highly involved in the exchange, but this response entails a minimization of the importance of the positive event, a focus on the potential downsides of the event, or both. Although the responder is actively involved in the interaction, he or she spends that energy pointing out unseen or nonexistent negative implications of the event and making the event seem not so great in the first place through other means. To convey this during your interview, ask questions and make comments about any potential negative aspects regarding the event. In addition, ask the interviewee exactly what is so "good" about this good event. Comments and questions such as "What's so good about that?" and "Sounds like that has its downsides as well" are examples of this type of probing. You may take some notes on the event. In short, try to be an active but questioning interviewer. If you find this type of response difficult, remember that your interview is for demonstration purposes only and you and your interviewee will be discussing your responses and the instructions later in the activity.

  Variation 1: You may think that students could be uncomfortable in the AD or even the PD role. It is fine to limit this exercise to the AC and PC conditions and then discuss the other two conditions later.

4. Have each interviewer pair off with one interviewee. Tell them that they have the next 5 minutes to complete the task and report back to the classroom on the discussion.

   Variation 2: You can have each interviewee be interviewed a second time about the same event by another interviewer who is assigned different instructions. You could also give out a second set of instructions to the interviewers and have them interview a different person. This allows for direct comparison of some of the responses.

5. When the exercise is complete, begin the discussion. Ask interviewees how they felt about the interaction and whether it was fun or felt good to talk about their events. You will likely get a variety of reactions. Next, reveal that each interviewer had specific instructions on how to conduct the interview, and have the interviewer show his or her interviewee which instructions they had. Continue your discussion of capitalization.

DISCUSSION
When a person shares his or her positive event, there are several ways in which the target of that capitalization attempt can react (see Gable, Reis, Impett, & Asher, 2004, for details on how this taxonomy was derived). Past research has found that these responses have two major dimensions: How active versus passive the response is, and how constructive versus destructive the response is. In terms of the active–passive dimension, the responder can show interest and involvement when the event is shared, or the responder can be reserved and subdued in his or her reply. In terms of the constructive–destructive dimension, the responder can be positive and supportive, or he or she can be negative and unsupportive. When these two dimensions are combined, there are four prototypes of responses to capitalization attempts, AC, PC, AD, and PC.

To give a concrete example, imagine that Jane comes home from her job in a software company and excitedly tells her partner, Jack, that her boss had called her into a meeting and assigned her to be the team leader for the development of a new cutting-edge product that has the potential to earn the company millions of dollars. An AC response from Jack might be "Wow, this is great news! Your skills and hard work are definitely paying off; I am certain that the promotion you want is just around the corner. What is the product?" A PC response could be a warm smile followed by a simple "That's nice, dear." An AD response might be "Wow, I bet the project will be complicated and difficult, are you sure you can handle it? It sounds like it might be a lot of work for potentially little payoff; maybe no one else wanted to lead the project. You will probably have to work even longer hours this month." A PD response might be "You won't believe what happened to me today," or "Are you going to pick up the dry cleaning, or is it my turn?"

In discussing this activity in class, it is often helpful to give students an example of a positive event that they can relate to as being important. Have them generate possible reactions that would fall into the four categories of capitalization (as in the above example). Students who were interviewed can then discuss with the class the experience of being interviewed in an AC, PC, PD, or AD style; did the interview style affect their feelings or thoughts about themselves, the event they discussed, and the person interviewing them? Students who served as interviewers can discuss what it was like to employ the style they were assigned and how the interview might have proceeded differently if they had been given either no instructions or one of the other three sets.

Research has clearly shown that only one type of response is good for the person who is capitalizing on the positive event: an AC response. Specifically, studies have found that when others respond to capitalization attempts in an active and constructive way, the person who shared the event experiences personal benefits (e.g., increases in well-being) and relationship benefits (e.g., greater relationship satisfaction). When others respond either passively or destructively, people do not reap the personal or relationship benefits of capitalizing and often experience stress and other negative emotions (Gable et al., 2004; Gable, Gonzaga, & Strachman, 2006). Research has also shown that active and constructive responses have these beneficial effects because the person who had shared the event reports feeling more understood, validated, and cared for by the partner. Passive or destructive responses are associated with decreased feelings of being understood, validated, and cared for. These three factors are called *perceived responsiveness* and have been shown to be extremely important to personal well-being and close relationship formation and growth (e.g., Murray, Holmes, & Collins, 2006; Reis & Shaver, 1988).[1]

---

[1]To better grasp this topic, instructors and students are encouraged to consult the following source: Gable and Reis (2010).

REFERENCES

Gable, S. L., Gonzaga, G., & Strachman, A. (2006). Will you be there for me when things go right? Supportive responses to positive event disclosures. *Journal of Personality and Social Psychology, 91,* 904–917. doi:10.1037/0022-3514.91.5.904

Gable, S. L., & Reis, H. T. (2010). Good news! Capitalizing on positive events in an interpersonal context. In M. Zanna (Ed.), *Advances in experimental social psychology, 42* (pp. 195–257). New York, NY: Elsevier Press. doi:10.1016/S0065-2601(10)42004-3

Gable, S. L., Reis, H. T., Impett, E., & Asher, E. R. (2004). What do you do when things go right? The intrapersonal and interpersonal benefits of sharing positive events. *Journal of Personality and Social Psychology, 87,* 228–245. doi:10.1037/0022-3514.87.2.228

Murray, S. L., Holmes, J. G., & Collins, N. L. (2006). Optimizing assurance: The risk regulation system in relationships. *Psychological Bulletin, 132,* 641–666. doi:10.1037/0033-2909.132.5.641

Reis, H. T., & Shaver, P. (1988). Intimacy as an interpersonal process. In S. Duck (Ed.), *Handbook of personal relationships* (pp. 367–389). Chichester, England: Wiley.

12 EMPATHY
PERSPECTIVE TAKING AND PROSOCIAL BEHAVIOR: CARING FOR OTHERS LIKE WE CARE FOR THE SELF

Michael W. Myers and Sara D. Hodges

Students given different perspective-taking instructions read about a person in need and then rate their feelings of psychological closeness and empathic concern (sympathy) toward that person, as well as their desire to help a similar group of people.

CONCEPT

This activity demonstrates how perspective taking can evoke prosocial behaviors among people.

MATERIALS NEEDED

All students read the same vignette about a series of unfortunate events that occur to a man named Jared, who is homeless. Half of the students first receive "objective" instructions (see Appendix 12.1) before reading the vignette, while the other half receive "perspective taking" instructions (see Appendix 12.2). You will also need to create a data-tally grid on the board or pass out tally sheets to students. Finally, you will need calculators (the ones found in mobile phones will work) or access to a spreadsheet program like Excel to determine the means for the two groups.

INSTRUCTIONS

Before the class activity, make copies of the two instruction sets, along with the vignette and questions (see Appendices 12.1 and 12.2 for sample worksheets). Make enough copies so that half of your class can receive each version of the instructions. Students should not know at the outset that different instructions sets are being distributed, so do not include the words "perspective-taking" or "objective" on the instructions.

You can introduce this activity by telling students that you are going to talk about how people think about and form impressions of others whom they encounter for the first time. Tell them to read the instructions and story about "Jared" carefully and to answer all of the questions afterward.

After the students have completed the questionnaires, either you or they will need to tally the data from their packets. Record students' "condition" (i.e., which set of instructions—perspective taking or objective—they received), plus their responses to

The authors thank Jeffrey Froh, Matt O'Laughlin, Rebecca Neel, Acacia Parks, and Carolyn Weisz for their help in developing this activity.

DOI: 10.1037/14042-013

the three questions that serve as dependent variables in this activity: the overlapping circles question, how much sympathy students report feeling toward Jared, and the rank students assign to the social issue of homelessness ("option D" on the questionnaire). There are several possibilities for tallying results (which is best depends on class size and the class's ability to compute means): (a) have students in the same condition work together to compute their group mean; (b) designate students to tally the means for each condition; (c) have students call out their responses for each question while you write them on the board, grouping them by condition; (d) use "i-clickers" or other classroom data collection devices; or (e) have students turn in the questionnaires, tally the data yourself outside of class, and bring the results to the next class.

DISCUSSION

Each item in the questionnaire (see Appendices 12.1 and 12.2) corresponds to a different outcome that has been empirically found to be affected by perspective taking.

First, students who received perspective-taking instructions should report greater *self–other overlap*—a "lessened self/other distinction" (Aron, Aron, Tudor, & Nelson, 1992), also described as a sense of oneness and "shared or interconnected identities with others" (Cialdini, Brown, Lewis, Luce, & Neuberg, 1997). After reducing the psychological distinction between ourselves and another person by perspective taking, we are more motivated to help that other person when he or she is in need.

Second, students who received perspective-taking instructions also should report greater *empathic concern* for the target person, which is measured in the exercise by the sympathy question. Increased feelings of empathic concern are reliably associated with helping that other person (Batson, 1991).

Third, in addition to perspective taking leading to increased motivation to help another person through increased self–other overlap and increased emotional empathy, this greater willingness to help can extend to an increased willingness to help others from the same *group* as the target of perspective taking (Batson, Chang, Orr, & Rowland, 2002). Thus, students in the perspective-taking group should also feel increased concern for the group—homeless people—that Jared represents.

In summary, perspective taking is expected to have three results: Relative to students who received "objective" instructions, students who received perspective-taking instructions should choose more overlapping circles to represent their relationship with Jared, report more empathic concern (in the form of sympathy) for Jared, and rank homelessness as a more important charity.

All three results are expected to work in concert, but in previous use, this activity sometimes produces differences between the two groups on just one or two of the measures. Even when results are in the "right" direction, mean differences between the two groups tend to be small and are often not statistically significant, especially when class size is small. In addition, closeness and sympathy for Jared may be fairly low—he is, after all, a stranger. If your students have some statistical training, the results can present an opportunity to discuss statistical significance and floor effects. Furthermore, in "real life," perspective taking does not always lead to helping. If the results for all three questions do not turn out as predicted, or even if they do, you may ask students to think about and discuss what might be some environmental, individual, or cultural factors that may have affected the results (or have them complete Question 3 from the Writing Component section that follows).

Have students write responses to the following questions:

1. Think about a time that you tried to take the perspective of another person. What was the situation? What prompted you to take this other person's perspective? What were the thoughts that went through your head as you tried to understand what that person was thinking and feeling?
2. Look at what you wrote down for Question 1. In general, what type of thought is more common: self-related thoughts (e.g., imagining yourself in the situation, identifying yourself with the other person, recalling self-information) or target-related thoughts (e.g., imagining the other person's situation, imagining how the other person felt)?
3. Perspective taking does not *always* lead to helping the other person or his or her group. When might perspective taking backfire? What do you think are some of the factors that might lead perspective taking to *decrease* people's motivations to help others?

This in-class activity demonstrates the benefits of using perspective taking to evoke prosocial behaviors among people, especially toward strangers in need. The activity also highlights reasons *why* perspective taking may lead to greater helping of others: Perspective taking evokes a feeling of psychological closeness with others as well as increased empathy/sympathy (specifically, empathic concern) toward others.[1]

REFERENCES Aron, A., Aron, E. N., Tudor, M., & Nelson, G. (1992). Close relationships as including other in the self. *Journal of Personality and Social Psychology, 63,* 596–612. doi:10.1037/0022-3514.63.4.596

Batson, C. D. (1991). *The altruism question: Toward a social–psychological answer.* Hillsdale, NJ: Erlbaum.

Batson, C. D., Chang, J., Orr, R., & Rowland, J. (2002). Empathy, attitudes, and action: Can feeling for a member of a stigmatized group motivate one to help the group? *Personality and Social Psychology Bulletin, 28,* 1656–1666. doi:10.1177/014616702237647

Cialdini, R. B., Brown, S. L., Lewis, B. P., Luce, C., & Neuberg, S. L. (1997). Reinterpreting the empathy–altruism relationship: When one into one equals oneness. *Journal of Personality and Social Psychology, 73,* 481–494. doi:10.1037/0022-3514.73.3.481

Davis, M. H., Conklin, L., Smith, A., & Luce, C. (1996). Effect of perspective taking on the cognitive representation of persons: A merging of self and other. *Journal of Personality and Social Psychology, 70,* 713–726. doi:10.1037/0022-3514.70.4.713

Hodges, S. D., Clark, B., & Myers, M. W. (2011). Better living through perspective taking. In R. Biswas-Diener (Ed.), *Positive psychology as a mechanism for social change* (pp. 193–218). Dordrecht, Netherlands: Springer Press. doi:10.1007/978-90-481-9938-9_12

---

[1]To better grasp this topic, instructors and students are encouraged to consult the following sources: Davis, Conklin, Smith, and Luce (1996); Hodges, Clark, and Myers (2011).

Appendix 12.1

Please read the following story. At the end, you will be asked some questions about it and the person whose story it describes.

While you read this story, make careful observations of the information about the person described in the paragraph. Try to be as objective as possible about what has happened to the person and how it has affected his life. To remain objective, do not let yourself get caught up in imagining what this person has been through and how he feels as a result. Just try to remain detached as you read.

Jared is 24 years old and has been homeless for roughly 4 months. Originally, he lived in Albany, Oregon, where he worked as an assistant manager at a restaurant. With his paycheck, he was able to afford to rent a one-room apartment and own a car, if barely. However, one night driving home after work, he was involved in a serious car accident with a drunk driver. Jared broke both legs and his car was totaled. Jared had insurance, but it did not come close to covering all of his medical expenses, and the other driver had no insurance of his own. With no savings and unable to work, Jared had to cover his costs using credit cards. Soon, Jared had maxed out his limit and was facing huge interest rates. On top of that, as a result of his inability to work for a long time, Jared lost his job at the restaurant, and finding a new job quickly was practically impossible because he did not have a car anymore. Due to this spiral of events, Jared could no longer afford his apartment, and he sold what few possessions he owned to pay his bills. Jared does not want to remain homeless, but it is very difficult for him to get out of the current cycle that prevents him from earning money and affording a place of his own to stay.

1. Please circle the picture that best describes your relationship with the person in the story.

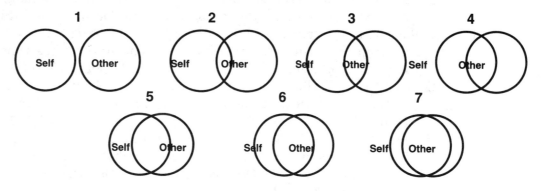

2. How much sympathy do you feel toward the person in the story?

None at all   A lot
1   2   3   4   5   6   7

Opinion Poll

You just read about a homeless person. We are curious about how important you think homelessness ranks compared with other social issues. Here is a list of current issues that have received media attention. Please rank the following charities in order of importance from "highest priority" to "lowest priority." That is, think about which of these you would recommend spending taxpayer money on or that you would donate money to yourself. Give a "1" to the charity that you think is the highest priority, "2" to the next highest priority, and so on, until you get to the charity that you think is the lowest priority, which you should give a "5."

RANK: (1 = *highest priority*; 5 = *lowest priority*)

_____ **a.** A program to assist developmentally delayed and disabled children with learning new skills.

_____ **b.** An advocacy and action group that works at the local level to protect and restore environmental resources.

_____ **c.** A center that provides language education and other support for immigrants.

_____ **d.** A human rights group that works to protect the rights and prevent the mistreatment of the homeless.

_____ **e.** A program that provides education, counseling, and social outlets for single parents.

Appendix 12.2

Please read the following story. At the end, you will be asked some questions about it, and the person whose story it describes.

While you read this story, try to take the perspective of the person described in the paragraph. Imagine what the person thinks and feels about what has happened to him and how it has affected his life. Concentrate on him in the experience. Think about his reactions. In your mind's eye visualize clearly and vividly how he feels in this situation. Try not to concern yourself with attending to all the information presented. Just imagine how Jared feels in this situation.

Jared is 24 years old and has been homeless for roughly 4 months. Originally, he lived in Albany, Oregon, where he worked as an assistant manager at a restaurant. With his paycheck, he was able to afford to rent a one-room apartment and own a car, if barely. However, one night driving home after work, he was involved in a serious car accident with a drunk driver. Jared broke both legs and his car was totaled. Jared had insurance, but it did not come close to covering all of his medical expenses, and the other driver had no insurance of his own. With no savings and unable to work, Jared had to cover his costs using credit cards. Soon, Jared had maxed out his limit and was facing huge interest rates. On top of that, as a result of his inability to work for a long time, Jared lost his job at the restaurant, and finding a new job quickly was practically impossible because he did not have a car anymore. Due to this spiral of events, Jared could no longer afford his apartment, and what few possessions he owned he sold to pay his bills. Jared does not want to remain homeless, but it is very difficult for him to get out of the current cycle that prevents him from earning money and affording a place of his own to stay.

1. Please circle the picture that best describes your relationship with the person in the story.

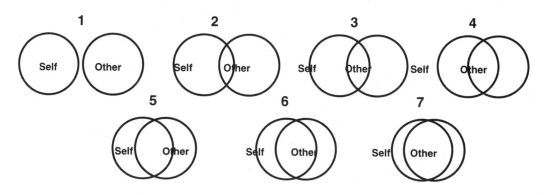

2. How much sympathy do you feel toward the person in the story?

None at all						A lot
1	2	3	4	5	6	7

Opinion Poll

You just read about a homeless person. We are curious about how important you think homelessness ranks compared with other social issues. Here is a list of current issues that have received media attention. Please rank the following charities in order of importance from "highest priority" to "lowest priority." That is, think about which of these you would recommend spending tax-payer money on or that you would donate money to yourself. Give a "1" to the charity that you think is the highest priority, and "2" to the next highest priority, and so on, until you get to the charity that you think is the lowest priority, which you should give a "5."

RANK: (1 = *highest priority*; 5 = *lowest*)

_____ **a.** A program to assist developmentally delayed and disabled children with learning new skills.

_____ **b.** An advocacy and action group that works at the local level to protect and restore environmental resources.

_____ **c.** A center that provides language education and other support for immigrants.

_____ **d.** A human rights group that works to protect the rights and prevent the mistreatment of the homeless.

_____ **e.** A program that provides education, counseling, and social outlets for single parents.

13 CULTURE AND SUBJECTIVE WELL-BEING CULTURE INFLUENCES THE INGREDIENTS OF A GOOD LIFE AND CONCEPTUALIZATIONS OF HAPPINESS

Christie Napa Scollon, Derrick Wirtz, and Xuan-yi Wei

This activity demonstrates how culture influences what people choose to emphasize in the good life by asking students to allocate points to different life priorities and to indicate their preference for activated versus deactivated positive emotions, after being primed with either an "individualistic" or "collectivistic" mind-set.

CONCEPT

You can consider several sources of information in deciding whether you are leading a highly satisfying life. Do you think about the pleasant feelings you experience frequently? Do you think about whether you are leading the kind of life that is approved of by your friends or parents? Whether people choose to rely on inner emotional experiences (e.g., the first question) or social information (e.g., the latter question) depends in part on their culture (Suh, Diener, Oishi, & Triandis, 1998). Much of the research on culture and subjective well-being has compared people from collectivist societies (e.g., China or Japan, where people usually define themselves in terms of their relationships with others) with people from individualistic societies (e.g., the United States, where people regard themselves as separate and distinct from others; Diener & Suh, 1999). Although there are certainly other ways to slice up the world (e.g., democracy vs. nondemocracy, developing vs. developed, tight vs. loose cultures), we focus on comparing individualist versus collectivist cultures in this chapter because we know the most about this comparison, in particular, how to activate each cultural framework. Because in any given classroom setting, all the students are likely to be from the same type of society, it does not make sense to compare collectivists and individualists. However, an analogous concept at the individual level is self-construal. The *independent self-construal* is much like that of an individualist, whereas the *interdependent self-construal* is like that of a collectivist. Although people's self-construals are related to the culture in which they live, importantly, for the purposes of this demonstration, people's self-construals can be temporarily manipulated to be more independent or interdependent. In this classroom demonstration, we prime members of a single culture to be more independent (individualistic) or interdependent (collectivist), and then we observe the differences in their life satisfaction judgments.

DOI: 10.1037/14042-014

Activities for Teaching Positive Psychology: A Guide for Instructors, J. J. Froh and A. C. Parks (Editors)

You will need copies of the thought-listing task V1 (independent self-construal prime) for half the class and copies of the thought-listing task V2 (interdependent self-construal prime) for the other half (see Appendices 13.1 and 13.2 for prompts). You will need one copy of the outcome measures (see Appendix 13.3) for each student. You will need a calculator to compute the mean score for each condition.

INSTRUCTIONS The thought-listing task is a self-construal priming task that was derived from ideas in Ybarra and Trafimow (1998) and Suh, Diener, and Updegraff (2008). Students receiving the independent self-construal prime are asked to write about what makes them different from their friends and family. Students receiving the interdependent self-construal prime are asked to write about what they have in common with their friends and family.

Upon completion of the listing task, all students will complete the outcome measures (see Appendix 13.3). The first outcome measure asks students to design their ideal life by using the "ingredients" listed. Each level of each ingredient costs that amount in "life bucks." The student designs his or her ideal life within a budget of 21 life bucks. The budget paradigm was derived from ideas in Li, Bailey, Kenrick, and Linsenmeier (2002). The idea behind it is that everybody would prefer to have high self-esteem, frequent pleasant emotions, constant social approval, and uninterrupted harmonious social relationships. The budget paradigm allows us to see what aspects people prioritize. Students might find the task difficult in the same way that shopping for an entire wardrobe on a $100 budget might be difficult.

The second outcome measure asks students to look at two different happy faces and select the one that represents true happiness. This item was derived from ideas in Tsai, Louie, Chen, and Uchida (2007). The closed-eyes, closed-mouth face looks more calm and contented (low arousal but pleasant), while the open-eyes, open-mouth face looks more excited (high arousal but also pleasant).

After the students complete the activity, the instructor should explain the difference between collectivist and individualist societies (Triandis, 1989) and independent and interdependent self-construals (Markus & Kitayama, 1991). Point out that the class received two different versions of the thought-listing task, and ask the class to guess which version was designed to prime the independent self and which was designed to prime the interdependent self. Ask students why thinking about one's uniqueness would prime the independent self-construal. Why does thinking about how one fits in with one's group prime the interdependent self-construal?

Next, tally responses for the independent and interdependent conditions separately. Compute the mean budget allocated to the feelings item and the mean budget allocated to the social approval item for the two construal groups separately. Table 13.1 illustrates the comparison.

Next, tabulate responses to the faces question separately for the two priming conditions. Table 13.2 illustrates the comparison.

DISCUSSION Did students in the independent condition give a greater allocation to feelings and a lesser allocation to social approval than did students in the interdependent condition, as expected? Ask students why personal feelings are given greater consideration in judgments of life satisfaction in an individualistic society and why social approval is given greater consideration in judgments of life satisfaction in a collectivist society. (In our experience with this task, no difference is usually found

Table 13.1 *Comparison Table for Life Bucks Allocation Task*

Budget allocation	Independent self-construal	Interdependent self-construal
Mean budget for *feelings*		
Mean budget for *social approval*		

Table 13.2 *Comparison Table for Face Selection Task*

Frequency	Independent self-construal	Interdependent self-construal
No. of students selecting Face A (low-arousal, positive affect)		
No. of students selecting Face B (high-arousal, positive affect)		

in budgets allocated to self-esteem, which is consistent with research showing that self-esteem is important to both collectivists and individualists; Kwan, Bond, & Singelis, 1997. We have also not found differences in budgets allocated to getting along with others, which is consistent with research showing the overwhelming importance of social relationships to personal happiness; Diener & Seligman, 2002.) How might the reliance on different cues (internal vs. social) affect overall levels of happiness? In other words, is it easier to be happy if you judge your happiness solely based on your internal cues? Some evidence from past research suggests that this is the case (Suh et al., 2008).

Did more students in the independent self-construal condition select Face B than Face A? Did more students in the interdependent self-construal condition select Face A than Face B? (If numbers of students in the two priming conditions were not equal, the instructor may need to compute percentages rather than use the raw counts.) Ask students to describe the emotions that are associated with each face. For example, Face A might bring to mind feelings of contentment and relaxation, while Face B might bring to mind feelings of pride and excitement. Ask students to list as many emotions as possible that go with each face and write them on the board in two columns. Students may even want to describe the events that might cause the different expressions. Discuss what the emotions under each face have in common. Which face displays higher arousal? Discuss with the students why people in collectivist societies might conceptualize life satisfaction more in terms of low-arousal positive emotions, while people in individualistic societies conceptualize life satisfaction more in terms of high-arousal positive emotions. Ask students to think of situations in which high-arousal positive states might be adaptive and situations in which low-arousal positive states might be adaptive. According to Tsai et al. (2006), influencing or persuading others involves high-arousal positive states (e.g., excitement), whereas adjusting to other people's needs and desires involves low-arousal positive states (e.g., calm, relaxed).[1]

---

[1]To better grasp this topic, instructors and students are encouraged to consult the following sources: Suh, Diener, Oishi, and Triandis (1998); Suh, Diener, and Updegraff (2008); and Tsai, Knutson, and Fung (2006).

REFERENCES

Diener, E., & Seligman, M. E. P. (2002). Very happy people. *Psychological Science, 13,* 81–84.

Diener, E., & Suh, E. M. (1999). *Culture and subjective well-being.* Boston, MA: MIT Press.

Kwan, V. S. Y., Bond, M. H., & Singelis, T. M. (1997). Pancultural explanations for life satisfaction: Adding relationship harmony to self-esteem. *Journal of Personality and Social Psychology, 73,* 1038–1051. doi:10.1037/0022-3514.73.5.1038

Li, N. P., Bailey, J. M., Kenrick, D. T., & Linsenmeier, J. A. W. (2002). The necessities and luxuries of mate preference: Testing the tradeoffs. *Journal of Personality and Social Psychology, 82,* 947–955. doi:10.1037/0022-3514.82.6.947

Markus, H. R., & Kitayama, S. (1991). Culture and the self: implications for cognition, emotion, and motivation. *Psychological Review, 98,* 224–253. doi:10.1037/0033-295X.98.2.224

Suh, E., Diener, E., Oishi, S., & Triandis, H. C. (1998). The shifting basis of life satisfaction judgments across cultures: Emotions versus norms. *Journal of Personality and Social Psychology, 74,* 482–493. doi:10.1037/0022-3514.74.2.482

Suh, E. M., Diener, E., & Updegraff, J. A. (2008). From culture to priming conditions: Self-construal influences on life satisfaction judgments. *Journal of Cross-Cultural Psychology, 39,* 3–15. doi:10.1177/0022022107311769

Triandis, H. C. (1989). The self and social behavior in differing cultural contexts. *Psychological Review, 96,* 506–520. doi:10.1037/0033-295X.96.3.506

Tsai, J. L., Knutson, B., & Fung, H. H. (2006). Cultural variation in affect valuation. *Journal of Personality and Social Psychology, 90,* 288–307. doi:10.1037/0022-3514.90.2.288

Tsai, J. L., Louie, J. Y., Chen, E. E., & Uchida, Y. (2007). Learning what feelings to desire: Socialization of ideal affect through children's storybooks. *Personality and Social Psychology Bulletin, 33,* 17–30. doi:10.1177/0146167206292749

Ybarra, O., & Trafimow, D. (1998). How priming the private self or collective self affects the relative weights of attitudes and subjective norms. *Personality and Social Psychology Bulletin, 24,* 362–370. doi:10.1177/0146167298244003

Appendix 13.1

In the spaces below, list the ways in which you are **different** from your family and friends.

1. _____
2. _____
3. _____
4. _____
5. _____
6. _____
7. _____
8. _____
9. _____
10. _____
11. _____
12. _____
13. _____
14. _____
15. _____

Wait—do not turn the page yet! Your instructor will let you know when to continue. Can you think of any more ways in which you are **different** from your family and friends?

Appendix 13.2

In the spaces below, list all the things you have **in common** with your family and friends.

1. _____
2. _____
3. _____
4. _____
5. _____
6. _____
7. _____
8. _____
9. _____
10. _____
11. _____
12. _____
13. _____
14. _____
15. _____

Wait—do not turn the page yet! Your instructor will let you know when to continue. Can you think of any more things you have **in common** with your family and friends?

Appendix 13.3

PART 1

In this task, we'd like you to design your <u>ideal life</u>.

In doing so, you will spend "life bucks" on different options.

For each of the options below, each desired level will cost you life bucks. For example, if you wish to experience high self-esteem 50% of the time, you will need to spend 5 life bucks.

The goal is to create the most satisfying life for you. However, you have to stick to the budget we have given you, and that is 21 life bucks. Make sure all of the numbers you have circled add up to 21.

Choose your ideal combination of the options below, for the ideal life. You have $21 in "life bucks" to use.	10% of the time				50% of the time					100% of the time
High self-esteem	$1	2	3	4	5	6	7	8	9	$10
Feelings such as *happiness, calm, excited, pleasant, proud, relaxed*	$1	2	3	4	5	6	7	8	9	$10
The approval of your friends and family	$1	2	3	4	5	6	7	8	9	$10
Getting along well with other people	$1	2	3	4	5	6	7	8	9	$10

Does your combination of options for your ideal life add up to 21? (circle one): YES / NO

PART 2 Which picture do you think best represents a person who is truly *happy and feels satisfied* with life?

CHOOSE ONLY ONE (circle your preference).

14 WEALTH AND SUBJECTIVE WELL-BEING SPENDING MONEY ON OTHERS LEADS TO HIGHER HAPPINESS THAN SPENDING ON YOURSELF

Lara B. Aknin and Elizabeth W. Dunn

Students will be asked to complete a short recall exercise in which they describe a recent purchase made for themselves or someone else and then report their current level of happiness. Students' happiness ratings will be examined to determine whether spending money on other people (prosocial spending) led to higher levels of happiness than spending money on oneself.

CONCEPT

Can money buy happiness? Does how you spend your money influence your well-being? Previous research has shown that simple spending choices with as little as $5 or $20 can lead to different happiness outcomes: Spending money on other people (prosocial spending) leads to higher levels of happiness than spending the same amount of money on oneself (personal spending). This classroom activity is designed to allow students to experience and replicate previous research by examining whether their own spending choices, such as spending $20 on themselves or someone else, leads to differences in happiness levels.

MATERIALS NEEDED

Each student will need a pen or pencil and should receive a recall questionnaire, along with one of the two memory prompts (see the appendices for samples). If possible, all personal spending memory questionnaires (see Appendix 14.1) should be printed on one shade of colored paper and all prosocial spending memory questionnaires (see Appendix 14.2) should be printed on a different shade of colored paper.

INSTRUCTIONS

For decades, researchers from psychology and economics have studied the fascinating relationship between money and happiness. The relationship was typically studied by using correlational designs and revealed a small but significant relationship between income and happiness, with the average correlation falling between .17 and .21 (Lucas & Dyrenforth, 2006).

Although this large body of research has demonstrated that income has a small but reliable association with well-being, new research has adopted a different approach to understanding how money affects happiness. For example, instead of examining the overall association between income and happiness, research in our lab has examined

DOI: 10.1037/14042-015
Activities for Teaching Positive Psychology: A Guide for Instructors, J. J. Froh and A. C. Parks (Editors)
Copyright © 2013 by the American Psychological Association. All rights reserved.

whether simple spending choices (i.e., *how* someone spends his or her money) influences people's well-being. Specifically, we have tested whether spending money on other people—*prosocial spending*—leads to higher levels of happiness than spending money on oneself (Dunn, Aknin, & Norton, 2008). In a series of studies, we found that participants who spent money on others were significantly happier than those who spent money on themselves. Thus, generous spending has been shown to produce higher levels of happiness than spending on oneself. More recently, we have found that simply *recalling* a previous act of prosocial spending can have similar effects. Specifically, in several recent studies, participants randomly assigned to describe a time they spent money on others were significantly happier than participants assigned to describe a time they spent money on themselves (Aknin et al., 2011). The classroom activity presented here allows students to replicate this research.

Before the activity, print one recall questionnaire for each student. Each student should receive only one type of questionnaire—either the personal or prosocial memory prompt—so print enough copies of each questionnaire for half your class (e.g., if you have 50 students, print 25 personal spending recall questionnaires and 25 prosocial spending recall questionnaires). When the questionnaires are printed, shuffle them so that the two recall questionnaires are mixed; this will provide an easy way to randomly assign students to one of the two recall conditions. Prepare three large sheets, the first labeled "1–3," the second, "4–6"; and the third, "7–9." Each label should be written in large, dark letters on a single 8 1/2" × 11" sheet of paper and posted at the front of the classroom.

In class, distribute an equal number of the personal and prosocial spending recall questionnaires. Tell students they will have 5 to 7 minutes to complete the recollection exercise and should then report their happiness ("How happy are you feeling right now?"; see the appendices for an example rating scale). While students describe their spending memory, mark the sheets labeled 1–3, 4–6, 7–9 to represent low, mid-range, and high happiness scores, respectively.

To avoid identifying or embarrassing students with low happiness scores, ask students to crumple their recall questionnaire into a paper ball. Then tell students to throw their paper ball to the front of the classroom and aim for the target that represents their happiness score. Check whether the data support the hypothesis by comparing the number and percentage of colored paper balls at the high end of the happiness scale. Support for the hypothesis would show a higher percentage of prosocial spending recall questionnaires at the high end of the happiness scale.

If you are unable to access colored paper for this classroom activity, variations of this exercise can make use of chalk boards, online forums, clickers, and raised hands. For instance, recall instructions can be posted on a chalk board in the classroom or online before class. Students could also complete this exercise at home and e-mail their happiness ratings to an instructor, who could compute an average happiness score for both the personal and prosocial spending recall groups. This activity can be adapted in many ways to suit your student and classroom needs.

DISCUSSION   The hypothesis tested in this class demonstration is that students who recall a time they spent money on others will report higher levels of happiness than students who recall a time they spent money on themselves. Discussion can center on whether this prediction was supported by the data. You may also want to read a few examples of personal and prosocial spending descriptions. Were students who recalled spending money on others happier? If so, why might this be? Were there any interesting examples of personal or prosocial spending? If the demonstration did not work, why might this be?

Can your students identify any potential confounding factors in the study design? For instance, might memories of prosocial spending lead to higher happiness because they involve spending time with others rather than spending money on others? Does recalling a spending experience accurately reflect how people feel immediately after they engage in these spending behaviors? Are there times when prosocial spending can backfire? What implications does this research have for individuals and society?[1]

REFERENCES

Aknin, L. B., Barrington-Leigh, C. P., Dunn, E. W., Helliwell, J. F., Burns, J. Biswas-Diener, R., . . . & Norton, M. I. (2011). *Prosocial spending and well-being: Cross-cultural evidence for a psychological universal.* Manuscript in preparation.

Dunn, E. W., Aknin, L. B., & Norton, M. I. (2008, March 21). Spending money on others promotes happiness. *Science, 319,* 1687–1688. doi:10.1126/science.1150952

Lucas, R. E., & Dyrenforth, P. S. (2006). Does the existence of social relationships matter for subjective well-being? In K. D. Vohs & E. J. Finkel (Eds.), *Self and relationships: Connecting intrapersonal and interpersonal processes* (pp. 254–273). New York, NY: Guilford Press.

---

[1]To better grasp this topic, instructors and students are encouraged to consult the following source: Dunn, Aknin, and Norton (2008).

Appendix 14.1

Please take 5 minutes to describe the last time you spent approximately $20 on yourself. While describing this spending event, you should reexperience the event as vividly as possible. In doing so, please think about how you felt at the time the event occurred and what led to those feelings.

_____

_____

_____

_____

_____

_____

_____

_____

_____

_____

How happy are you feeling right now?

1	2	3	4	5	6	7	8	9

Not at all
happy

Very
happy

Appendix 14.2

Please take 5 minutes to describe the last time you spent approximately $20 on some-one else. While describing this spending event, you should reexperience the event as vividly as possible. In doing so, please think about how you felt at the time the event occurred and what led to those feelings.

_____

_____

_____

_____

_____

_____

_____

_____

_____

_____

How happy are you feeling right now?

_____

1	2	3	4	5	6	7	8	9

Not at all
happy

Very
happy

15 MINDFULNESS CULTIVATING MINDFULNESS THROUGH LISTENING

Shauna L. Shapiro and Timothy R. Mariels

This exercise is designed to elicit a firsthand experience of mindfulness through intentional listening and sharing. Students speak in front of a group of their peers and attempt to maintain a mindful awareness of that experience as it is happening.

CONCEPT

Although the concept of mindfulness is most often associated with Buddhism, it is conceptualized as a universally applicable practice and an innate human capacity. *Mindfulness* is "the awareness that arises through intentionally attending in an open, caring, and discerning way" (Shapiro & Carlson, 2009, p. 4). Mindfulness cultivates both attention and presence and can be defined as "paying attention in a particular way: on purpose, in the present moment, and nonjudgmentally" (Kabat-Zinn, 1994, p. 4). In combination, these facets of mindfulness are intended to remove barriers and allow one to see clearly by embracing the broad spectrum of human experience.

Mindful awareness is described as a way of relating to all experience—positive, negative, and neutral—in an open, receptive way. This awareness involves freedom from grasping and from wanting anything to be different. It simply knows and accepts what is here, now. Thus, mindfulness involves simply knowing what is arising as it is arising without adding anything to it—without trying to get more of what we want (pleasure, security) or pushing away what we do not want (e.g., fear, anger, shame).

Shapiro and Carlson (2009) developed a model of mindfulness comprising three core elements: intention, attention, and attitude (IAA). *Intention* refers to knowing why we are practicing mindfulness and understanding our personal vision and motivation. *Attention* involves observing the operations of one's moment-to-moment, internal and external experience. *Attitude* refers to the qualities one brings to attention and includes a general sense of openness, acceptance, curiosity, and kindness. It is helpful to use the IAA model of mindfulness when facilitating the small-group activity of mindful listening. The instructor invites students to reflect on their intention to listen carefully to what each student shares, by paying attention to the present moment, with an open, curious, and kind attitude.

Mindfulness has been demonstrated to decrease depression, anxiety, and diverse stress-related disorders (Brown & Ryan, 2003) and to increase self-efficacy, happiness,

DOI: 10.1037/14042-016
Activities for Teaching Positive Psychology: A Guide for Instructors, J. J. Froh and A. C. Parks (Editors)
Copyright © 2013 by the American Psychological Association. All rights reserved.

empathy, spirituality, and life satisfaction (Shapiro, Schwartz, & Santerre, 2002). Instructors can gain a greater understanding of the basic tenets of mindfulness and how it has the ability to manifest well-being by reading Shapiro, Carlson, Astin, and Freedman (2006) and Brown and Ryan (2003).

MATERIALS NEEDED

It is essential for you to define mindfulness clearly to your students before engaging the class in the mindful listening activity. You should then hand out the Reflection Questions (see Appendix 15.1) to be answered in small groups after the exercise.

INSTRUCTIONS

Invite students to share three things with the class: (a) first name, (b) one thing that is stressful in their lives, and (c) one thing they are grateful for. The exercise is most effective if the desks and students are arranged a circle or semicircle. Instruct each student to share all three things with the class as a whole. Students should speak one at a time, beginning at one end of the circle or semicircle. Each student speaks approximately 1 to 2 minutes. Remind the students before beginning that the exercise is not about the content of what they share but about the process of cultivating and experiencing mindfulness.

Tell students to pay attention to how it feels to speak, how it feels to share something stressful, and how it feels to share something for which they are grateful. Invite them to notice body sensations, thoughts, and emotions as they share and as they listen. It is helpful to remind students that this is an exercise in practicing "mindfulness" and to invite them to set an intention before beginning the exercise. An intention is similar to a goal; however, it is not outcome oriented, in the sense that it is more of a direction than a destination. Here are examples of potential intentions the instructor can offer to the class: "May I stay present as I am listening," "May I be open and accepting," and "May I notice and let go of any judgments of myself or others." It is important for students to notice their attitudes toward speaking, about what they are sharing, and how they are listening and paying attention as those around them share.

Once the mindfulness exercise is completed, ask students to break into groups of three. Then invite them to answer the discussion/reflection questions in Appendix 15.1, focusing on their direct experience of the mindful listening exercise. Give students 5 to 7 minutes for their small-group discussions. Then bring the groups back together and lead a larger class discussion drawing on the students' direct experience during the mindful listening exercise as well as the small-group discussions. Encourage students to share their specific personal experiences and to expand on the small-group conversations. It can be helpful to have each small group choose a group leader to report to the larger group what was discussed and what was found to be most prevalent, unique, or interesting. At the end of the larger group discussion of the exercise, you can use the discussion suggestions below to expand the students' understanding of mindfulness and the methods that encompass mindful practice and its study.

DISCUSSION

Students often report that they find it difficult to pay attention and listen to the other students around them because they are rehearsing what they going to say when it is their turn. It is often especially difficult to pay attention to the other students speaking just before their turn. The mind wants to prepare, and so listening, paying attention, and staying present become challenging. Another common reaction of students is that after they have shared, they often have trouble mindfully listening to the next student because they are preoccupied with reviewing how they did and often judging themselves for not being "good enough." It is helpful for the instructor to highlight this self-judgment and to help students cultivate a more accepting and compassionate stance toward themselves. The mindful listening exercise is an excellent example of how we often miss the present moment because we are concerned about the future (e.g., what am I going to share) or preoccupied with the past (e.g., I did not share appropriately, I should have said this instead of that). Instead of listening, there is often planning; instead of hearing, there is often judgment about how well the student perceived he or she did the exercise.

Another important dimension to highlight in discussion is to bring awareness to students' body sensations during the exercise: "What did you notice in your body as you were speaking, immediately before you spoke, after you spoke?" It is helpful for students to become aware of what it feels like to be nervous, excited, or relieved. It is also useful to inquire about how it felt as students were listening to each other (e.g., "Did you feel connected, empathic, bored, distracted, concerned?") and to connect these emotions to sensations in the body.

It is especially important to continue bringing students back to the present moment and back to mindful awareness even during the discussion process. For example, after a student shares or responds, it is helpful to pause and have him or her notice how it feels to be speaking now, bringing attention to process as opposed to content. The exercise is not about what students share, but about their relationship to what is arising in the present moment.

WRITING COMPONENT

There are several writing options that can build on and enhance this exercise. You can have the students answer only three of the reflection questions in the appendix during the exercise and write the rest of the answers separately. It is helpful to remind students of their intention for the listening exercise and to have them reflect on how this influenced their capacity to listen. In addition, students can reference their direct experience in the exercise and write about which concepts were most integral to their moment-to-moment awareness. They can use the optional writing exercise to share more personal experiences that they might not feel comfortable in sharing with the rest of the class.[1]

REFERENCES

Bien, T. (2006). *Mindful therapy: A guide for therapists and helping professionals.* Boston, MA: Wisdom.

Brown, K. W., & Ryan, R. M. (2003). The benefits of being present: Mindfulness and its role in psychological well-being. *Journal of Personality and Social Psychology, 84,* 822–848. doi:10.1037/0022-3514.84.4.822

Cordon, S. L., Brown, K. W., & Gibson, P. R. (2009). The role of mindfulness-based stress reduction on perceived stress: Preliminary evidence for the moderating role of attachment style. *Journal of Cognitive Psychotherapy, 23,* 258–269. doi:10.1891/0889-8391.23.3.258

---

[1]To better grasp this topic, instructors and students are encouraged to consult the following sources: Bien (2006); Brown and Ryan (2003); Cordon, Brown, and Gibson (2009); Germer, Siegel, and Fulton (2005); Goldstein and Kornfield (1987); Salzberg (1995); Segal, Williams, and Tisdale (2002); Shapiro et al. (2006); Shapiro and Carlson (2009); and Siegel (2007).

Germer, C., Siegel, R., & Fulton, P. (Eds.). (2005). *Mindfulness and psychotherapy*. New York, NY: Guilford Press.

Goldstein, J., & Kornfield, J. (1987). *Seeking the heart of wisdom: The path of insight meditation*. Boston, MA: Shambhala.

Kabat-Zinn, J. (1994). *Wherever you go, there you are: Mindfulness meditation in everyday life*. New York, NY: Hyperion.

Salzberg, S. (1995). *Lovingkindness: The revolutionary art of happiness*. New York, NY: Shambhala.

Segal, Z., Williams, J., & Tisdale, J. (2002). *Mindfulness-based cognitive therapy for depression*. New York, NY: Guilford Press.

Shapiro, S. L., & Carlson, L. E. (2009). *The art and science of mindfulness: Integrating mindfulness into psychology and the helping professions*. Washington, DC: American Psychological Association. doi:10.1037/11885-000

Shapiro, S. L., Carlson, L. E., Astin, J. A., & Freedman, B. (2006). Mechanisms of mindfulness. *Journal of Clinical Psychology, 62*, 373–386. doi:10.1002/jclp.20237

Shapiro, S. L., Schwartz, G. E. R., & Santerre, C. (2002). Meditation and positive psychology. In C. R. Snyder (Ed.), *Handbook of positive psychology* (pp. 632–645). New York, NY: Oxford University Press.

Siegel, D. J. (2007). *The mindful brain: Reflection and attunement in the cultivation of well-being*. New York, NY: Norton.

Appendix 15.1

Reflection Questions:

1. How did it feel to speak during the mindful listening exercise?
2. How did it feel to listen during the mindful listening exercise?
3. Did you notice your mind wandering away from the present moment? What pulled your attention away?
4. How did you bring your attention back to the present moment?
5. Did you notice your mind judging what you or others said? How did "judging" feel in your body?
6. Did you notice moments of feeling connected, empathic toward others? How did this feel in your body?
7. Did you notice any specific sensations in your body right before you spoke? Right afterward?
8. What are you feeling, experiencing right now after the mindful listening exercise?
9. Were you able to bring the attitudes of acceptance, curiosity, kindness to your attention?
10. What do you think would happen if you practiced mindful listening with each person you spoke to? How would it feel if you set the intention to pay attention with curiosity, kindness, and acceptance to everything you said and everything you listened to? Do you think mindful listening would change the way you interact and relate with others?

16 FORGIVENESS
TEACHING FORGIVENESS IN POSITIVE PSYCHOLOGY

Everett L. Worthington Jr., Aubrey L. Gartner,
David J. Jennings II, and Don E. Davis

Students participate in and learn to lead a psychoeducational group for an evidence-based psychological practice to promote forgiveness.

CONCEPT
This in-class activity helps students learn about forgiveness by applying it to their own lives. They participate in a psychoeducational group based on the REACH forgiveness model (Worthington, 2006) to help them forgive someone against whom they are holding a grudge. Eight students are in a "fishbowl," which is an inner circle of active participants. The rest of the students are in an outer circle and participate in all group exercises but do not talk during inner-circle processing of the exercises. The activity is aimed at promoting leadership so that undergraduates can lead such groups in dormitories, community and church groups, and other venues.

MATERIALS NEEDED
Students are directed to a website (http://www.people.vcu.edu/~eworth) containing leader and participant manuals for the evidence-based REACH forgiveness intervention (Worthington, 2003, 2006). The manuals may be downloaded, modified, and used at no cost. Manuals for both secular and explicitly Christian universities are available, and a training DVD is available through the first author.

INSTRUCTIONS
A 1-hour minilecture on forgiveness precedes the activity—either earlier in the course or in the class immediately preceding the activity. All four of us who have taught positive psychology courses at Virginia Commonwealth University teach this module as follows. Because many students conceptualize forgiveness within the context of an injustice and struggle with whether forgiveness can be done responsibly, we begin with a discussion of retributive justice and restorative justice (Zehr, 1995). Whereas the objective of *retributive justice* is punishment of the offender for wrongs committed, *restorative justice* focuses on restoring the offender to the community, usually after making some *reparation* for wrongdoing (i.e., restitution, apology, and seeking forgiveness and reconciliation explicitly). We often use the characters of Inspector Javert and Jean Valjean from *Les Misérables* as illustrations of retributive and restorative justice, respectively. To tie justice to the concept of forgiveness, we suggest assigning a discussion question (e.g., "Based on your understanding of forgiveness and justice, write a

DOI: 10.1037/14042-017
Activities for Teaching Positive Psychology: A Guide for Instructors, J. J. Froh and A. C. Parks (Editors)

paragraph on how you think they relate to each other"). The key point to highlight in this discussion is that justice, which is interpersonal, is not opposed to forgiveness, which occurs within the person. For instance, a person might forgive a burglar, but forgiveness does not affect whether the apprehended burglar might be convicted of a crime.

Next, we delve into the concept of forgiveness itself and suggest that there are two kinds of forgiveness, both of which will be learned through participating in the psychoeducational group. Both refer to ways of coping with the interpersonal stressors of hurt or offense (for a summary, see Worthington, 2006). *Decisional forgiveness* is a decision about one's behavioral intentions. One replaces negative intentions with intentions to eschew revenge and to treat the offender as a person of value and worth. Students grant decisional forgiveness through imagining that they are holding their grudge tightly in their outstretched arms as the leader talks of the heavy burden of carrying around a grudge. Students are invited to release the grudge and let it fly away. *Emotional forgiveness* is the emotional replacement of unforgiving emotions with positive other-oriented emotions, such as empathy, sympathy, compassion, and love. Students spend the bulk of their time doing exercises (like an "empty chair" conversation in which they imagine conversing with the offender) grouped in five clusters prompted by the acronym REACH (described below).

We suggest that the best way to understand the two types of forgiveness and how emotional forgiveness takes place through emotional replacement of negative unforgiving emotions is to participate in a psychoeducational in-class group. We invite all students to participate in two class sessions in which the teacher conducts the group. We discuss people's thoughts and feelings about forgiving and suggest that forgiveness is not for everyone. Thus, we permit people who are opposed to forgiving to observe the forgiveness groups from the outer edge of a fishbowl and to participate only in the exercises with which they feel comfortable.

The intervention teaches the REACH forgiveness model, which is an evidence-based treatment that is backed by more than 10 randomized clinical trials and has been used and tested in a variety of other settings independently. REACH is an acronym that helps participants remember the principles of the intervention (R = *recall* the hurt without rancor, E = *emotional replacement* of unforgiving emotions with positive emotions, A = *altruistic gift* of forgiveness given to the offender, C = *commit* to the forgiveness experienced, H = *hold onto* forgiveness experienced). The intervention involves experiential activities to promote each step. Students are assigned to familiarize themselves with the manuals before the first class on forgiveness.

We recommend performing this activity during a 3-hour class period in which the professor models leadership of a forgiveness intervention by running an abbreviated forgiveness group using a fishbowl method and the students learn forgiveness (and incidentally how to run such groups) by participating in the group. (The professor should review the manual in advance and select activities to include based on the time available.) Eight students volunteer to be the small group at the center of the fishbowl. The leader facilitates the intervention for all students. However, only students in the fishbowl participate in discussion of activities. Those outside the fishbowl are encouraged to observe how the leader introduces activities, transitions between activities, reinforces key principles of the interventions, and facilitates brief discussions aimed at enhancing the effectiveness of the intervention.

Activities involve a sampling of the experiential exercises in the manual for each step in the REACH model. Each group leader (i.e., the teacher or, later, students who have gone through the group) can design his or her own group by selecting exercises to fill available group time from over 19 hours of exercises. The creator of the model recommends which exercises are crucial, but the leader can select others on the basis of preference. The final 30 minutes of the intervention involves writing that is aimed at helping participants generalize their learning of the model. Students identify 10 offenses they have experienced during their past. They write a brief summary of each (e.g., "My father refused to let me attend the prom because I had missed a curfew the month before"). The leader narrates a set of questions that has students apply and practice the REACH forgiveness model to several of those offenses (e.g., "Write how you might empathize with the person who offended you"). Although students write during the activity, this is not a "writing activity" that can be evaluated; rather, it is a personal experience that happens to be done in writing. After the activity is completed, students discuss (a) their experience in the group and (b) their observations about leadership. Most students report substantial forgiveness by the end of the intervention and report increased confidence that they could lead a similar group.

DISCUSSION

One issue that often comes up in the discussion of forgiveness is students' concerns that forgiveness may not always be well advised. They might ask, What if forgiveness is expected of one but not felt? Or, conversely, What if expressing forgiveness leads to repeat offenses? It is important, then, to highlight that *feeling* forgiveness and deciding to forgive are not the same as *expressing* forgiveness. They can be independent of one another. One might say one forgives merely to set an offender up for retribution (i.e., expressing forgiveness without deciding to forgive or feeling forgiveness), or one might internally forgive for one's own benefit, yet not express that forgiveness so that the offender continues to feel guilty (i.e., feeling forgiveness without expressing it). We emphasize that forgiveness as an internal experience is possible regardless of the social situation; however, it may indeed often not be well advised to express no-strings-attached forgiveness, especially if the offender is likely to reoffend.

Forgiveness, likewise, is not the same as *reconciliation*, which is the interpersonal restoration of trust in a relationship. Forgiveness thus depends on two people both being trustworthy. This distinction is important to highlight when students bring up examples such as an abusive spouse, where one might worry that forgiveness prevents an individual from leaving a dangerous circumstance. Students often are concerned about this issue in the context of situations in their own lives or in the lives of their loved ones, so it is likely to surface at some point during the process.

Other students embrace forgiveness as an application of their religious beliefs and practices (Worthington, 2003). We encourage such applications, but we also describe forgiveness as a human, secular enterprise (Worthington, 2006). Forgiveness is a big umbrella.

Forgiveness, we emphasize, is not a panacea. Intrapersonally, it has substantial benefits in promoting physical and mental health and in helping people restore relationships. For many, there are also spiritual benefits of forgiving. In this brief exercise, we help people learn (a) forgiveness in the context of justice; (b) distinctions among decisional forgiveness, emotional forgiveness, communicating forgiveness, and reconciliation;

(c) how to forgive more quickly and thoroughly if they wish to do so; and (d) how to lead informal groups to help others forgive.[1]

REFERENCES

Fehr, R., Gelfand, M. J., & Nag, M. (2010). The road to forgiveness: A meta-analytic synthesis of its situational and dispositional correlates. *Psychological Bulletin, 136*, 894–914. doi:10.1037/a0019993

Hall, J. H., & Fincham, F. D. (2005). Self-forgiveness: The stepchild of forgiveness research. *Journal of Social and Clinical Psychology, 24*, 621–637. doi:10.1521/jscp.2005.24.5.621

Miller, A. J., Worthington, E. L., Jr., & McDaniel, M. A. (2008). Forgiveness and gender: A meta-analytic review and research agenda. *Journal of Social and Clinical Psychology, 27*, 843–876. doi:10.1521/jscp.2008.27.8.843

Wade, N. G., Worthington, E. L., Jr., & Meyer, J. (2005). But do they really work? Meta-analysis of group interventions to promote forgiveness. In E. L. Worthington, Jr. (Ed.), *Handbook of forgiveness* (pp. 423–440). New York, NY: Brunner-Routledge.

Wiesenthal, S. (1998). *The sunflower: On the possibilities and limits of forgiveness* (Rev. and expanded ed.). New York, NY: Schocken.

Worthington, E. L., Jr. (2003). *Forgiving and reconciling: Bridges to wholeness and hope.* Downers Grove, IL: InterVarsity Press.

Worthington, E. L., Jr. (2006). *Forgiveness and reconciliation: Theory and application.* New York, NY: Brunner-Routledge.

Worthington, E. L., Jr., Witvliet, C. V. O. Pietrini, P., &; Miller, A. J. (2007). Forgiveness, health, and well-being: A review of evidence for emotional versus decisional forgiveness, dispositional forgivingness, and reduced unforgiveness. *Journal of Behavioral Medicine, 30*, 291–302. doi:10.1007/s10865-007-9105-8

Zehr, H. (1995). *Changing lenses: A new focus on crime and justice.* Scottdale, PA: Herald Press.

[1]To better grasp this topic, instructors and students are encouraged to consult the following sources: Fehr, Gelfand, and Nag (2010); Hall and Fincham (2005); Miller, Worthington, and McDaniel (2008); Wade, Worthington, and Meyer (2005); Wiesenthal (1998); and Worthington, Witvliet, Pietrini, and Miller (2007).

17

FLOW
FLOW AND OPTIMAL
LEARNING ENVIRONMENTS

David J. Shernoff and Brett Anderson

In this activity, students participate in the leading methodology used to research flow (the experience sampling method) by tracking and graphing their subjective experiences when signaled in a variety of instructional activities throughout an instructional unit on flow and engagement in learning.

CONCEPT

Flow is a peak experiential state of focused concentration and elevated enjoyment during intrinsically interesting activities. The experience of flow is further characterized by deep absorption, the perception of being in control, loss of self-consciousness, and a distorted perception of time (usually time seems to fly). It is suggested that students first obtain instruction in the basic concept and theory of flow through readings, presentations, or discussions before initiating the activity described in this chapter (suggested readings are provided below). The purpose of the activity is to introduce students to the principal research method for studying flow, the experience sampling method (ESM), and in the process allow students to monitor their level of flow and other subjective perceptions.

MATERIALS NEEDED

The primary materials needed are an electronic device to make multiple alarm sounds and self-report surveys for students to complete when signaled by the alarm. In previous ESM research (see Hektner, Schmidt, & Csikszentmihalyi, 2007), Casio wristwatches equipped with multiple alarms were preprogrammed for signaling respondents, but any device that makes an alarm sound, such as most cell phones, may be used so long as the instructor has determined in advance when to signal the class. A random number generator (several can be found online) can aid in identifying a random time during the activity to signal the class. When signaled, students complete a brief paper-and-pencil survey regarding their subjective experience in the moment just before the signal. Students are provided with a packet of at least five or six customized experience sampling forms (ESFs), one for each activity in which the class is signaled. (See Appendix 17.1. The ESF is a common survey used in this type of research; see Hektner et al., 2007, for additional examples.) In recent years, researchers have experimented with devices that allow respondents to complete ESFs electronically, such as student response systems (i.e., "clickers"). One advantage of these systems is direct data entry by the participant. A disadvantage, however, may be increased completion time, which is particularly undesirable during instruction.

DOI: 10.1037/14042-018
Activities for Teaching Positive Psychology: A Guide for Instructors, J. J. Froh and A. C. Parks (Editors)

It is suggested that students first be exposed to presentations and readings for background in how and why various aspects of activities are expected to contribute to flow experiences (e.g., Csikszentmihalyi, 1990; Strati, Shernoff, & Kackar, in press). For example, a common property of flow activities is that one knows exactly what needs to be done and how to accomplish it. Once a clear goal is established, what is needed to maintain flow as the activity unfolds is immediate and continual feedback on how well one is doing with respect to reaching the goal. The central theoretical criterion for flow to occur is a high level of skill use to meet a significant challenge presented by the activity. Thus, the activity should neither be too easy nor impossibly difficult; ideally, it is challenging but attainable. The emphasis is more on the process than the product, a process in which the individual feels autonomous and in control through the employment of sufficient skills. The perception of importance or meaningfulness and being active instead of passive have also been found to predict engagement in learning based on the flow model (Shernoff & Csikszentmihalyi, 2009).

Research suggests that students' levels of flow and engagement with learning fluctuate by pedagogical conditions (Shernoff & Csikszentmihalyi, 2009). Therefore, in this activity the instructor signals the students in the class at a random time point while the students are engaged in each of a variety of learning activities throughout an instructional unit on flow and/or student engagement. At the signal, the students complete an ESF. To observe variations in their levels of flow and engagement in learning, it is suggested that students be signaled during at least one high-flow activity and one low-flow activity. Instructors may wish to experiment with creating high- and low-flow activities. Typically, low-flow activities include many common noninteractive, whole group presentations (e.g., lectures), videos, or other activities in which students are relatively passive. High-flow activities are typically structured, challenging, and purposeful, and they solicit the use of students' skills.

One example of a high-flow activity for students is to apply and extend the concept of flow into educational or learning environments based on the premise that flow experiences provide an experiential foundation of engagement with learning. This activity provides students with practice as future educators or practitioners in designing and creating the conditions that allow youths to experience flow. Designing environmental conditions that facilitate flow for a target population, such as children or adolescents, is essential in promoting healthy development as well as meaningful learning experiences (Shernoff, 2011). To design this high-flow activity, divide the classroom into groups of five or six students. Then, tell the students that they will apply their knowledge of flow to a real-world situation to support youth development. Provide each group with written instructions that specify a unique population and context around which the group is to design a flow-inducing activity. In our pilot of this activity, example populations included high school students, middle school students, middle school girls, and late adolescents (e.g., ages 17–22); examples of contexts included an after-school club, an art class, a mentoring program to promote resiliency and leadership, a civic action program to promote citizenship and awareness of societal issues, and a computer science class. This diversity of scenarios is intended to push the limits of the class's collective knowledge about how educators would create flow. The remaining instructions direct each group to identify and describe (a) *the activity*, (b) *defining rules* of the activity, (c) *instructions* for the population, (d) *the goals* of the activity, (e) *infusion of flow conditions*, and (f) how the group will know if the activity indeed facilitated flow (i.e., *method of evaluation*). Each student in the group is to be responsible for describing one of these components on a blank sheet of paper by the end of the 35- to 40-minute period, followed by a group discussion.

Once the instructional unit and all of the activities have been completed, provide instructions for students to fill in their ESF ratings on a data table or chart. For example, students can record all of their ratings on a single item (e.g., challenge) in one row of a table, including a note about what activity they were doing at the time of the signal. It is especially instructive to graph the data over the course of the unit. Students simply draw a line graphing their ratings on a single item during each of the activities to see how it varied by activity type and flow conditions. To structure the activity further, graph templates may be prepared in advance numbering each activity and labeling it a high-flow or a low-flow activity. In addition to tracking their ratings of concentration, interest, and enjoyment in activities separately, students can create a composite measure of engagement on the basis of flow theory by calculating the average of these three ratings at the time of each signal (Shernoff & Csikszentmihalyi, 2009). Draw students' attention to how their pattern of engagement (and perceived learning) varied as their perception of challenge, skills, or other flow conditions fluctuated with each activity, as can be demonstrated by graphing these variables on the same graph. An example graph using the actual data from one student in our class when we piloted this activity is provided in Figure 17.1.

DISCUSSION If indeed ESM data reveal that students are more engaged in high-flow activities, as in our example, it should not escape notice that this was likely because the conditions for flow were more salient in such activities. The example high-flow activity described above was designed to (a) provide a sense of autonomy and control though designing an

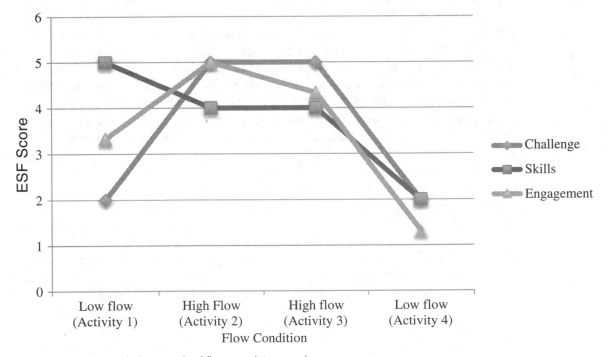

Figure 17.1.   Example line graph of flow conditions and engagement.

original flow activity and choosing roles; (b) provide a clear goal for each student (i.e., through the specification of individual roles and responsibilities); (c) provide a challenge demanding the use of skills, requiring focused concentration to complete within the time given; (d) provide feedback to each individual from the supervising instructor as well as student collaborators; (e) solicit a variety of skills (e.g., social, verbal, written) and interests; and (f) foster interactivity conducive to "group flow." The contributions of such conditions in creating flow may be identified and discussed with students in processing the ESM data from the activity.

In piloting the use of the ESM during a unit on flow and student engagement, we utilized a variety of activity types, including lecture/presentation, videos, small- and large-group discussions, written reflections, and structured writing activities (see Writing Component). It was expected that higher engagement would be reported during individual and group work (e.g., the high-flow activity described above and the structured writing activity) as a result of the solicitation of skill use, concentration, and other flow conditions designed into the activity. An analysis of the ESM data collected in our pilot study revealed that perceptions of challenge and skill were indeed significantly higher in these activities than in the others. The engagement composite (i.e., mean of concentration, interest, and enjoyment) was also significantly higher in the writing activity than in the other activities. Engagement was higher in the high-flow activity than in the lecture/presentation activities, but this difference was not statistically significant. Overall, however, *optimal learning environments* were created when conditions for flow and engagement with learning were intentionally designed, as in the high-flow activity described above (Shernoff, 2011).

Despite the variation in subjective experience students reported during the unit, we wondered whether a larger increase in flow and engagement occurs in activities that are situated outside of the classroom that connect with students' lives and interests in the "real world" (Shernoff, 2011). Thus, in the following semester in the same course, we created a service learning class project to involve students with a real-life initiative to create a service-oriented student organization on campus. Again, the ESM was administered in a range of activities that included presentations and videos on innovative community service organizations for youth, the creation of a student organization on campus, outreach efforts to attract membership, and the production and distribution of promotional materials. An analysis of the data suggested that situating activities in the real world did not trump the other factors theorized to produce flow, however. In fact, engagement was significantly higher during the flow unit in the first semester than during the community service class project in the second ($F = 3.16$, $p < .01$). One exception to this trend was that students reported elevated engagement in the second semester during highly structured and interactive service learning group activities to increase awareness of issues such as violence and oppression. Our interpretation is that these were the only activities in which the conditions for flow such as skill use and clear goals were created to a similar extent as in the high-flow activity described earlier.

The reasons that students did not report higher engagement or conditions for flow in the community service class project were left open to interpretation. One reason may be that the goal of the project was not necessarily the students' own goal but rather imposed by the instructor; thus, there was significant variation in the degree to which students aligned with the goal. If so, it is clear that making an instructional goal clear is not the same thing as individual students having a clear goal for themselves as in *autotelic* activities (Csikszentmihalyi, 1990). Second, learning about and applying flow are found by many students to be inherently novel and interesting topics, an interpretation supported by the reflective written comments in the first semester.

A third interpretation is that the experience of engagement and flow in the moment measures only students' immediate emotional and affective reactions and is separate from larger, more global meaning making at the core of students' valuations of their educational experiences. In the second semester, most students demonstrated an understanding of how community service was of value to adolescent development. Results of surveys and reflections further revealed that most students felt that working toward social change and making a difference in their community or in the world were important, personally meaningful, and made them feel good about themselves. Overall, these observations were consistent with one of the tenets of positive psychology that two of the three "routes to happiness," other than the pursuit of pleasure, are engagement (e.g., flow) and meaning (i.e., the pursuit of something larger than one's self; Parks, Schueller, & Tasimi, in press).

WRITING COMPONENT

Following the unit on flow, students write written responses to the following questions:

1. What did you learn about flow, or flow in the life of adolescents, that was most valuable?
2. Do you think that the ESM (i.e., beeper) method accurately captured your level of flow and engagement over the course of the unit? Why or why not?
3. Would there be a better way? If so, what?

DISCUSSION

In this activity, students simultaneously (a) learn about the concept of flow, its relation to learning, and how to apply it to create optimal learning environments; (b) gain an understanding of a leading methodology used to study flow and student engagement (i.e., ESM); and (c) experience heightened engagement during activities in which conditions for flow were present. As students record and process their ESM data, the conditions most important for creating flow can be identified and discussed. In this manner, students learn and experience the concept of flow and have an opportunity to practice positive psychology.

Overall, this study illustrates some benefits of a research design situated in the context of educational psychology instruction. Through the process, students' understanding may be deepened. As students record and process their ESM data, for example, the conditions most important for creating flow may be identified and discussed. Instruction and research become interactive and continually inform each other to help students not only learn but also *practice* educational psychology.[1]

REFERENCES

Csikszentmihalyi, M. (1990). *Flow: The psychology of optimal experience.* New York, NY: Harper Perennial.

Hektner, J. M., Schmidt, J. A., & Csikszentmihalyi, M. (2007). *Experience sampling method: Measuring the quality of everyday life.* Thousand Oaks, CA: Sage.

---

[1]To better grasp this topic, instructors and students are encouraged to consult the following sources: Csikszentmihalyi (1990); Shernoff and Csikszentmihalyi (2009); Strati, Shernoff, and Kackar (2012).

Parks, A. C., Schueller, S., & Tasimi, A. (in press). Increasing happiness in the general population: Empirically supported self-help? In I. Boniwell & S. David (Eds.), *Oxford handbook of happiness.* Oxford, England: Oxford University Press.

Shernoff, D. J. (2011). Engagement and positive youth development: Creating optimal learning environments. In K. R. Harris, S. Graham, & T. Urdan (Eds.), *The APA educational psychology handbook: Vol. 2. Individual differences and cultural and contextual factors* (pp. 195–220). Washington, DC: American Psychological Association.

Shernoff, D. J., & Csikszentmihalyi, M. (2009). Flow in schools: Cultivating engaged learners and optimal learning environments. In R. C. Gilman, E. S. Heubner, & M. J. Furlong (Eds.), *Handbook of positive psychology in schools* (pp. 131–145). New York, NY: Routledge.

Strati, A. D., Shernoff, D. J., & Kackar, H. Z. (2012). Flow. In R. Levesque (Ed.), *Encyclopedia of adolescence* (pp. 1050–1059). New York, NY: Springer.

Appendix 17.1

Experience Sampling Form

Instructions. You will be signaled four times over the course of the unit on flow and student engagement. Each time you are signaled, please complete the below seven items by circling your response. You will be reminded which activity number it is.

Activity number_____

	Not at all	A little	Somewhat	Pretty much	Very much
1. How **important** was this activity or topic to you and your goals?	1	2	3	4	5
2. Was it **interesting**?	1	2	3	4	5
3. Was it **challenging**?	1	2	3	4	5
4. Did you **enjoy** what you were doing?	1	2	3	4	5
5. How hard were you **concentrating**?	1	2	3	4	5
6. Were you using a high level of **skill**?	1	2	3	4	5
7. How much were you **learning**?	1	2	3	4	5

III
SELF-REFLECTIONS

PURPOSE

Activities in this part ask students to do something inside or outside the classroom that provides firsthand experience with the relevant concept; students then reflect on that experience and share their reflections with the class.

OVERVIEW OF ACTIVITIES

In **Gratitude**, by Philip C. Watkins, Amy Sparrow, and Amy C. Webber, students apply a gratitude technique to cope with an unpleasant memory. Todd B. Kashdan and Paul J. Silvia offer an exercise that explores the role of **Curiosity** in social interactions, drawing students' attention to the interplay between curiosity and anxiety as they engage in a social activity. In their chapter on **Happiness Promotion**, Jaime L. Kurtz and Sonja Lyubomirsky offer "mindful photography"—taking pictures of situations, places, and people that evoke a target emotional or cognitive state—as a way of giving students hands-on experience with how research on happiness interventions is commonly done. In her chapter on **Hope**, Jeana L. Magyar-Moe outlines a process by which students identify a goal, explore that goal and how they might best pursue it, and create a project comprising verbal and visual representations of their goal as a way of fostering hope; these projects are mailed to students by the instructor after the class has ended as a way of rekindling the hope that may have faded over time. **Materialism**, a trait associated with lower well-being, is highlighted by Yuna L. Ferguson and Tim Kasser with an activity called the "media fast," where students avoid commercial media for several days and reflect on the impact that commercial media have on their pursuit of materialistic goals. Patrick R. Harrison, Jennifer L. Smith, and Fred B. Bryant provide students with an in-depth exploration of the experience of **Savoring** by asking them to orchestrate a "savoring expedition" and reflect on their experience. Kennon M. Sheldon helps students apply self-determination theory to understand their own **Motivation** in the classroom. To engender civic **Engagement**, Constance Flanagan and Brian D. Christens ask students to write an op-ed piece on a civic or community issue.

18

GRATITUDE
TAKING CARE OF BUSINESS WITH GRATITUDE

Philip C. Watkins, Amy Sparrow, and Amy C. Webber

This activity demonstrates how grateful coping can help bring closure to troubling memories and how this can be an important facet in explaining how gratitude contributes to the good life. In this activity, students write about an unpleasant memory in a manner that helps them gratefully reappraise that memory. Following the writing exercise, students assess closure and the emotional impact of the memory.

CONCEPT

Gratitude has been shown to be one of the strongest correlates of emotional well-being, and experimental studies have supported the theory that gratitude enhances happiness (Watkins, Van Gelder, & Frias, 2009). This activity demonstrates one of the mechanisms whereby gratitude enhances well-being: grateful coping. In this exercise, students will write about a painful memory in a manner that helps them reframe the memory to help bring closure and decrease the unpleasant emotional impact of the memory.

MATERIALS NEEDED

Although students can complete this exercise using their own materials (blank sheets of paper and writing utensils), we think that it is better to provide the journaling materials, including the outcome measures and the journaling instructions (see Appendix 18.1). Presentation slides of the results from Watkins, Cruz, Holben, and Kolts (2008) will assist in your discussion of the exercise (see Figures 18.1, 18.2, and 18.3).

INSTRUCTIONS

Although there are probably several mechanisms whereby gratitude enhances well-being (for a review, see Watkins et al., 2009), some research suggests that one of the strongest explanations is that grateful people deal particularly well with difficult events. Grateful people are probably good at reframing negative events in memory in such a way as to decrease their unhealthy impact. We like to present this exercise in the context of discussing gratitude mechanisms that might enhance happiness.

At least one day or one lecture before conducting this activity, you should prepare your students for this exercise. In an announcement, you should inform them that they will be asked to recall and write about an unpleasant *open memory*, and you should describe the nature of open memory. This announcement serves two purposes: It provides an appropriate preparation for the exercise and helps students come to the

DOI: 10.1037/14042-019
Activities for Teaching Positive Psychology: A Guide for Instructors, J. J. Froh and A. C. Parks (Editors)
Copyright © 2013 by the American Psychological Association. All rights reserved.

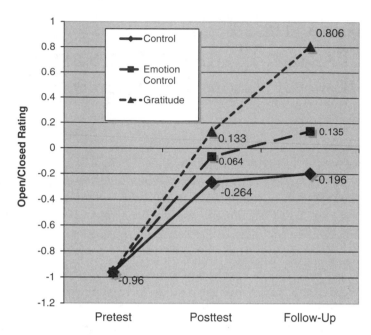

Figure 18.1. Estimated marginal means of memory openness by writing condition and test. Higher scores indicate more closure. From "Taking Care of Business? Grateful Processing of Unpleasant Memories," by P. C. Watkins, L. Cruz, H. Holben, and R. L. Kolts, 2008, The Journal of Positive Psychology, 3, p. 93. Copyright 2008 by Routledge. Adapted with permission.

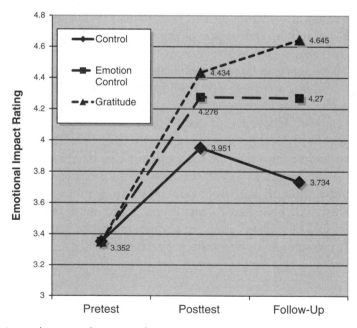

Figure 18.2. Estimated marginal means of emotional impact of memory by writing condition and test. Higher scores indicate more pleasantness. From "Taking Care of Business? Grateful Processing of Unpleasant Memories," by P. C. Watkins, L. Cruz, H. Holben, and R. L. Kolts, 2008, The Journal of Positive Psychology, 3, p. 93. Copyright 2008 by Routledge. Adapted with permission.

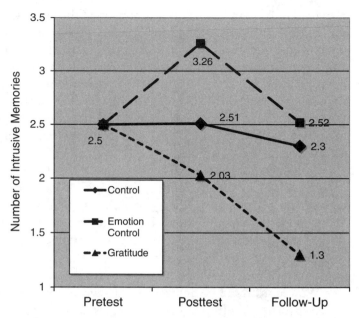

Figure 18.3. Estimated marginal means of number of intrusive open memories by writing condition and test. From "Taking Care of Business? Grateful Processing of Unpleasant Memories," by P. C. Watkins, L. Cruz, H. Holben, and R. L. Kolts, 2008, The Journal of Positive Psychology, 3, *p. 94. Copyright 2008 by Routledge. Adapted with permission.*

demonstration with the painful memory that they can work with during the exercise. The following is a suggested announcement:

> On (date) we will conduct a gratitude exercise in which you will be asked to recall an "open memory" from your past. This is a negative emotional memory that you feel has some "unfinished business" associated with it. This memory should not be too traumatic or too personal (e.g., please avoid memories of abuse), but any unpleasant memory that you feel that you do not understand well and that continues to bother you would be appropriate. For example, many students recall episodes of romantic rejection, disappointing academic performance, or incidents of regret. After you recall this memory, I am going to ask you to write about it in a way that should help you deal with it.

Although this reframing exercise may have value in helping people deal with deeply traumatic memories, we feel that reappraising very traumatic memories in this way is probably better accomplished under the guidance of a therapist, rather than in class.

On the actual occasion of the demonstration, first hand out the exercise packet (see Appendix 18.1). Next, ask students to recall their open memory. After students have written down their memories, ask them to report on the openness and emotional impact of the memory (see Appendix 18.1).

The next step is to have your students begin the journaling exercise. We like to have the journaling instructions written down for our students, but we think it is also good to read the instructions in Appendix 18.1 aloud. (Feel free to provide students with extra blank pages if needed.)

After 20 minutes, inform the students that they can stop their journaling and that they may now complete the questions on the following page. An optional aspect of this exercise is to provide your students with the real-time intrusive memory measure that is provided in Appendix 18.1. In this portion of the exercise, students are to recall as "many *positive* events as you can from anytime in your past" for 3 minutes. If, however, their open memory comes to mind during this task, they are to check a box at the bottom of the page. Because the students' task is to recall positive events, the coming to mind of an open memory is an incidence of an intrusive memory. One of the characteristics of open memories is that they tend to be intrusive, that is, they invade consciousness at times when they are unwelcome. Having students engage in this aspect of the exercise will give them a good understanding of the intrusive memory results that you will discuss following this exercise.

A discussion of students' experiences with the demonstration should follow this activity. First, we recommend encouraging students to continue the exercise outside of class. In most expressive writing paradigms, three journaling sessions, 20 minutes each, are used, and in the study that this demonstration is based on (Watkins et al., 2008), we used three sessions on consecutive days. Often students will carry the activity discussion themselves, but there are a few issues that we think should be emphasized for this demonstration to provide a complete learning experience.

We recommend beginning the discussion by asking students about their experience with the grateful reappraisal exercise and their perception of the outcome of this exercise. Following are some questions that might help guide discussion:

- As you wrote about your memory, what kinds of facts about your unpleasant event became prominent?
- Were there new facts about the event that you recognized?
- As you thought in this new way about the event, how did you feel?
- Did you find yourself experiencing new emotions about the event?
- How has the meaning of this event changed for you?
- How has the significance of this event changed?
- How does this event fit into your life story?
- Have you learned anything new about yourself?
- How has this writing exercise changed you?
- Do you think that this might change how you act in the future?

For the most part, this discussion can take place without students divulging the content of the painful experience that they recalled. Some students will report significant gains in their understanding of this painful event, although many will not see any notable effect. This may be because, as in other positive psychology interventions, something similar to a sleeper effect seems to occur with this intervention.

We found that the largest gains from the grateful reappraisal intervention occur in the week *after* the intervention. This is why we feel that it is important to discuss the results of Watkins et al. (2008) after completing this exercise. Briefly, in our study we randomly assigned participants to one of three journaling conditions in which they wrote for 20 minutes on 3 consecutive days. In our two comparison conditions, participants either wrote about their plans for the following day, or in the emotion control condition they wrote about the unpleasant event itself. In the critical grateful reappraisal condition, students wrote about outcomes of the event that they could now feel grateful for. Our results are presented in Figures 18.1 through 18.3. In Figure 18.1, higher numbers indicate more closure. In Figure 18.2, higher numbers indicate more pleasant impact of the memory. Numbers of intrusive memories of the critical event are shown in Figure 18.3. We recommend presenting these graphs during your discussion of the exercise. You will need to describe the comparison conditions from this study for the students to fully understand these graphs. Students seem to gain a personal understanding of these outcomes fairly easily because they have just completed the gratitude journaling activity.

This exercise illustrates several issues that usually produce fruitful discussions in class. For example, as explained above, the results of this study illustrate the sleeper effects that are sometimes found in positive psychology interventions (e.g., *using signature strengths* and *recalling three good things*; see Seligman, Stern, Park, & Peterson, 2005). This contrasts with the treatment effects that are often found in traditional clinical psychology, where the benefits of treatment usually show declines after the conclusion of treatment. Another issue that this exercise effectively demonstrates is *closure*. Often issues of closure are discussed in the context of clinical psychology, but unfortunately this valuable construct is not fully defined. Here, we feel that the work of Beike and her colleagues (e.g., Beike & Wirth-Beaumont, 2005) provides a good discussion that helps move forward our understanding of "bringing closure" to issues in therapy. In this context, we have also found that this demonstration provokes interesting discussion of *pleasant open memories*. Whereas it is probably important to bring closure to negative open memories, might positive open memories actually enhance well-being? Although we know of no research that speaks to this issue, we have found this to be an enjoyable discussion topic for students.

DISCUSSION

There are other gratitude exercises that we feel should be used in positive psychology courses as well as the one we described here. Demonstrations that use the "counting blessings" type of exercise (e.g., Emmons & McCullough, 2003; Seligman et al., 2005) and the "gratitude visit" (Seligman et al., 2005) have been used successfully in positive psychology courses. Because these interventions are well known and adequately described elsewhere, we chose to present this "taking care of business" exercise.

In the study that this activity is based on (Watkins et al., 2008), we found that grateful reappraisal of unpleasant open memories results in more closure, decreased unpleasant emotional impact, and decreased intrusiveness of these memories. Although evidence seems to support the theory that gratitude is an important facet of the good life, very little is known about *how* gratitude promotes well-being. We have found that a presentation of putative gratitude mechanisms for well-being provokes good discussion in positive psychology courses, and we believe that the activity we have described here provides an effective demonstration of how grateful coping enhances the good life.[1]

---

[1]To better grasp this topic, instructors and students are encouraged to consult the following sources: Beike and Wirth-Beaumont (2005); Emmons and McCullough (2003); Seligman et al. (2005); Watkins et al. (2008).

REFERENCES Beike, D. R., & Wirth-Beaumont, E. T. (2005). Psychological closure as a memory phenomenon. *Memory, 13*, 574–593. doi:10.1080/09658210444000241

Emmons, R. A., & McCullough, M. E. (2003). Counting blessings versus burdens: An empirical investigation of gratitude and subjective well-being in daily life. *Journal of Personality and Social Psychology, 84*, 377–389. doi:10.1037/0022-3514.84.2.377

Seligman, M. E. P., Steen, T. A., Park, N., & Peterson, C. (2005). Positive psychology progress: Empirical validation of interventions. *American Psychologist, 60*, 410–421. doi:10.1037/0003-066X.60.5.410

Watkins, P. C., Cruz, L., Holben, H., & Kolts, R. L. (2008). Taking care of business? Grateful processing of unpleasant memories. *The Journal of Positive Psychology, 3*, 87–99. doi:10.1080/17439760701760567

Watkins, P. C., Van Gelder, M., & Frias, A. (2009). Furthering the science of gratitude. In R. Snyder & S. Lopez (Eds.), *Oxford handbook of positive psychology* (2nd ed., pp. 437–445). New York, NY: Oxford University Press.

Appendix 18.1

Now I would like you to bring to mind an open memory. An *open memory* is a troubling memory from your past that you feel is not yet behind you and is poorly understood. It is an emotional memory that may intrude into your consciousness at unwelcome times, and you feel you have some "unfinished business" associated with this memory. In other words, in many ways this emotional memory is still an "open book" for you. On the lines on the first page of your packet, write several sentences about the event you have recalled.

_____

_____

_____

_____

Please rate your open memory on the following attributes:

How open/closed would you say the memory you recalled is? (Please circle a number.)

Unfinished business (Very Open)			Neither open or closed			Closed Book
−3	−2	−1	0	1	2	3

How does recalling this memory *affect you now*?

1	2	3	4	5	6	7	8	9
very negative effect	strong negative effect	moderate negative effect	slight negative effect	no effect at all	slight positive effect	moderate positive effect	strong positive effect	very positive effect

Please wait until your instructor tells you to continue to the next page.

Please recall your open memory again. For the next 20 minutes I would like you to write about your open memory. Think again about this experience for a few moments. At first it may seem that the event you wrote down might not have had any positive effects on your life. However, sometimes even when bad things happen, they ultimately have positive consequences, things we can now be grateful for. Try to focus on the positive aspects or consequences of this difficult experience. As the result of this event, what kinds of things do you now feel thankful or grateful for? How has this event benefited you as a person? How have you grown? Were there personal strengths that grew out of your experience? How has the event made you better able to meet the challenges of the future? How has the event put your life into perspective? How has this event helped you appreciate the truly important people and things in your life? In sum, how can you be thankful for the beneficial consequences that have resulted from this event? As you write, do not worry about punctuation or grammar, just really let go and write as much as you can about the positive aspects of your experience that you feel you now can be grateful for.

_____

_____

Please wait until your instructor tells you to continue to the next page.

Now I would like to ask you some more questions about your ***open memory***.

How open/closed would you say the memory you recalled is? (Please circle a number.)

Unfinished business (Very Open)			Neither open or closed			Closed Book
−3	−2	−1	0	1	2	3

How does recalling this memory ***affect you now***?

1	2	3	4	5	6	7	8	9
very negative effect	strong negative effect	moderate negative effect	slight negative effect	no effect at all	slight positive effect	moderate positive effect	strong positive effect	very positive effect

For the next 3 minutes we would like you to briefly list as many *positive* events as you can from anytime in your past. Each number represents a different life event. Just write a short sentence describing the event. If, while trying to think of positive events from your life, you actually remember the open memory you wrote about on the previous page, check one of the boxes provided at the bottom of the page. Check a box each time you think of your open memory. Remember, your primary task is to **list as many positive events that you can think of from any time in your past.**

Event	Event
1.	17.
2.	18.
3.	19.
4.	20.
5.	21.
6.	22.
7.	23.
8.	24.
9.	25.
10.	26.
11.	27.
12.	28.
13.	29.
14.	30.
15.	31.
16.	32.

Every time your open memory comes to mind, check a box below:

☐ ☐ ☐ ☐ ☐ ☐ ☐ ☐ ☐ ☐ ☐ ☐

☐ ☐ ☐ ☐ ☐ ☐ ☐ ☐ ☐ ☐ ☐ ☐

19

CURIOSITY
CURIOSITY AS A SOCIAL LUBRICANT: TRANSFORMING CONVERSATIONS TO BE INTERESTING, ENGAGING, AND MEANINGFUL

Todd B. Kashdan and Paul J. Silvia

For this activity, students experience curiosity and exploratory behavior, how curiosity and anxiety work together, and how curiosity can be helpful in improving the quality of social interactions. After developing an important question, students circle the room and ask each other their questions, thus creating conditions for observing the interplay of curiosity and anxiety as well as the interpersonal value of curiosity.

CONCEPT   This experiential exercise assists people in understanding curiosity; the relationship between anxiety and curiosity; and how curiosity can be used to generate more enjoyable, interesting, and meaningful social interactions and relationships.

MATERIALS NEEDED   Each person needs one piece of paper and a pen, pencil, crayon, stylus, or quill and ink.

INSTRUCTIONS   Perhaps the students have read articles about curiosity beforehand (see References), or perhaps they have never read anything on this topic. Regardless, this activity should take place before any discussion about the nature of curiosity.

While everyone is seated, ask the students to write down one question, idea, or thought that they would want to talk about with someone in a conversation. Ask them to consider the mundane small talk that permeates most conversations. Ask them to think about their ideal stimulating conversations. Ask them to write down a question that would interest them, a question that they crave to know how somebody else would answer. Encourage them to be flexible and open with their ideas. Let them know that feeling anxious and uncertain is perfectly normal during this exercise. Encourage them to be self-compassionate instead of censoring what they are thinking for being silly, bizarre, or inappropriate. Give them permission to let their thoughts go where they go and, when they are ready, to write the question that they wish they were talking about with other people. Ask them to fold the piece of paper.

That was the first part of the exercise. Before they do anything else, give students the following instructions:

- In a moment, you are going to get up, with that question in your hand, and mindfully stroll around the room. I am going to give you gentle instructions while you

DOI: 10.1037/14042-020
Activities for Teaching Positive Psychology: A Guide for Instructors, J. J. Froh and A. C. Parks (Editors)

stroll. Do not say a word as you are walking around the room until I say so. Now, please stand up and stroll.

- While you are moving around, pay attention to how you move. Notice what you are feeling. Notice what you are thinking. Notice what you are doing. Look at the people you are passing without talking. In a minute, I am going to ask you to stop, face another person, and hand that person the paper in your hand. Take turns. One person reads and answers the question, and then you switch. Keep in mind that the person giving you that paper cares about what he or she wrote; this question was important to him or her. Be open and receptive to what the other person wrote and respond in an open, generous way.
- Introduce yourself and then take turns with the questions in your hands. (It doesn't matter whether students remain standing or seated, just give them autonomy to do this exercise their own way.)

As the students are talking, sit back and observe from a distance. Expect this to go on for 5 to 10 minutes. If there is high energy in the room, let the discussion go on. The debriefing will make the time worthwhile if it goes on for an extra 5 or so minutes. When you notice that a few people stopped talking to each other, get everyone to stop the task. But do so gently. If they are standing, ask them to return to their seats. Comment on the energy or lack of energy in the room. Then enter the debriefing stage.

Ask them the following questions, elaborating on answers given.

- What was going through your mind as you decided on the question you were going to ask?
- What was going through your mind as you were told that you were going to use it in an actual conversation with someone in the room?
- What were you thinking and feeling as you walked around the room before I asked you to stop and talk?
- How did it feel to be asked questions?
- Who asked closed-ended questions? I want to explore what happened. Who asked open-ended questions? What, if anything, happened differently?
- Who ran out of things to talk about? Could you share what happened and why the conversation came to a halt?
- As your conversation unfolded, did you feel less anxious? What feelings replaced anxiety?
- How was this like or unlike your everyday conversations?
- Why aren't we talking about what we are interested in?
- What is one lesson that you can take away from this exercise to use in your daily life?

During the debriefing portion, look for information on the emotions that people had before, during, and after the exercise. Look for individual differences (e.g., extraversion, agreeableness, anxiety sensitivity, trait curiosity) and situational factors (e.g., talking to someone of a different gender or race/ethnicity) that influenced people's emotions and behavior. For instance, ask students to raise hands if they tend to be extraverted and how many had positive experiences (do the same for students defining themselves as introverted). What the research shows is that during one-on-one interactions, introverted people are visibly similar to extraverted people in terms of sociability, positivity, and disclosure (Fleeson, Malanos, & Achille, 2002). How students responded to the exercise provides an opportunity to discuss this research. Curiosity tends to be relatively independent of people's degree of extraversion or introversion.. Moreover, in a strong or intense situation such as the one created in this exercise, personality tends to exert a weaker influence (Mischel & Shoda, 1995). Use the actual responses from students to discuss these research findings. If the responses in this class do not fit with these research findings, try to uncover why. Ask the students and then give your own interpretations (e.g., small sample, might have been different at a party instead of in a college classroom setting).

Look for blended emotions, particularly for instances where students felt curious and anxious at the same time. The most intense, enduring pleasures often occur when we feel energized and positive, but also a little bit anxious/uncomfortable (Kashdan, 2009). Think of first dates, roller coasters, horror movies, and accomplishing a difficult task. This is a good opportunity to explore whether it makes sense to refer to "positive" emotions as those that are pleasant and "negative" emotions as those that are unpleasant. A different approach is to think of positive emotions as those that are helpful, and in this case, anxiety is often a positive emotion. Talk about the transition to the classroom and whether students felt let down that the activity was over. Talk about carryover effects and how they might influence the desire to talk to partners in the future and maybe initiate a friendship.

DISCUSSION   Use this exercise as a transition to discussing existing theory and research on curiosity (see References). Walk the students through the relationship between curiosity and anxiety. Discuss how curiosity and anxiety are the two main ways people respond to novelty: new, challenging, and unexpected things can evoke curiosity and the desire to explore as well as anxiety and the desire to escape (Silvia & Kashdan, 2009). Being a curious person thus means not only cultivating curiosity but also managing and accepting anxiety and uncertainty. In terms of a well-lived life, we have to be attuned to how we respond to these approach–avoidance conflicts. We can learn to change how we respond, and it starts with a single decision to remain in situations and explore them even when they make us feel anxious and uncomfortable (Kashdan & Steger, 2007). In terms of understanding intimacy, investment, and commitment in relationships, being curious when partners share positive events appears to be as important as (if not more important than) being supportive when partners share negative events. Discuss how the science of curiosity provides evidence for a mind-set and psychological strength with relevance to building healthy social relationships.[1]

REFERENCES   Fleeson, W., Malanos, A., & Achille, N. (2002). An intraindividual, process approach to the relationship between extraversion and positive affect: Is acting extraverted as "good" as being extraverted? *Journal of Personality and Social Psychology, 83,* 1409–1422. doi:10.1037/0022-3514.83.6.1409

---

[1]To better grasp this topic, instructors and students are encouraged to consult the following sources: Kashdan (2009); Kashdan et al. (in press); Kashdan, McKnight, Fincham, and Rose (2011); Silvia (2006).

Kashdan, T. B. (2009). *Curious? Discover the missing ingredient to a fulfilling life.* New York, NY: William Morrow.

Kashdan, T. B., Dewall, C. N., Pond, R. S., Silvia, P. J., Lambert, N. M., Fincham, F. D., . . . Keller, P. S. (in press). Curiosity protects against interpersonal aggression: Cross-sectional, daily process, and behavioral evidence. *Journal of Personality.*

Kashdan, T. B., McKnight, P. E., Fincham, F. D., & Rose, P. (2011). When curiosity breeds intimacy: Taking advantage of intimacy opportunities and transforming boring conversations. *Journal of Personality, 79,* 1369–1402. doi:10.1111/j.1467-6494.2010.00697.x

Kashdan, T. B., & Steger, M. F. (2007). Curiosity and pathways to well-being and meaning in life: Traits, states, and everyday behaviors. *Motivation and Emotion, 31,* 159–173. doi:10.1007/s11031-007-9068-7

Mischel, W., & Shoda, Y. (1995). A cognitive-affective system theory of personality: Reconceptualizing situations, dispositions, dynamics, and invariance in personality structure. *Psychological Review, 102,* 246–268. doi:10.1037/0033-295X.102.2.246

Silvia, P. J. (2006). *Exploring the psychology of interest.* New York, NY: Oxford University Press. doi:10.1093/acprof:oso/9780195158557.001.0001

Silvia, P. J., & Kashdan, T. B. (2009). Interesting things and curious people: Exploration and engagement as transient states and enduring strengths. *Social and Personality Psychology Compass, 3,* 785–797. doi:10.1111/j.1751-9004.2009.00210.x

20

HAPPINESS PROMOTION
USING MINDFUL PHOTOGRAPHY TO INCREASE
POSITIVE EMOTION AND APPRECIATION

Jaime L. Kurtz and Sonja Lyubomirsky

Students use a camera to help them identify and capture things in their lives that are meaningful or positive, and subsequent class discussions can touch on topics of appreciation, savoring, happiness, and the underlying mechanisms that may make this activity effective. Moreover, the activity can be used to illustrate how empirical research on increasing happiness is commonly done.

CONCEPT

Research in positive psychology has convincingly demonstrated that people can sustainably increase their happiness by using effortful cognitive and behavioral strategies (Lyubomirsky, Sheldon, & Schkade, 2005). One novel classroom activity that can be used to enhance happiness is mindful photography. Other research suggests that this activity leads to boosts in positive mood and enhanced savoring or appreciation of one's immediate physical environment and one's life in general (Bryant, Smart, & King, 2005). Preliminary data show that students find the activity engrossing, enjoyable, and thought provoking; indeed, they report it to be more enjoyable than the well-studied activity of counting one's blessings (Kurtz, 2011). As a classroom activity, mindful photography fits most naturally into lessons on hedonic adaptation, savoring, gratitude, and happiness-increasing strategies. However, as described here, it can easily be modified to complement a variety of topics within courses in positive psychology.

MATERIALS NEEDED

Each student will need either a digital camera or a cellular phone with a camera. In our experience, nearly all students have one or both of these or can easily borrow one.

INSTRUCTIONS

In all variations of the mindful photography activity, students should receive written instructions, such as the following:

> Throughout the course of the day today, you will take photographs of your everyday life. As you do this exercise, think about the things in your life that bring you happiness or joy. What brings you positive feelings in your daily life? Although this is highly personal, some examples might include your favorite scenic view on campus, your closest friends, or your favorite book. Have your camera or camera phone handy and take at least five photographs of such things today. It is important to take the activity seriously and not rush through it.

The activity should be done in advance of the class it is designed to complement so that students arrive in class ready to share their impressions and reactions. This

---

DOI: 10.1037/14042-021

Activities for Teaching Positive Psychology: A Guide for Instructors, J. J. Froh and A. C. Parks (Editors)

version of the activity is designed to focus on positive emotions; however, the activity is rather unconstrained, with students being allowed to choose their own subject matter. Instructors should feel free to modify the instructions to suit their purposes. For example, to supplement a discussion on appreciation of natural beauty, instructors may ask students to photograph objects outdoors. We suggest they take five photographs, as this number is sufficiently high to be involving but not so high that the photography becomes a chore. As described later, instructors could vary this number slightly or test which number is optimal for their students.

Rather than focusing explicitly on topics that bring them happiness, the mindful photography exercise can be varied by having students photograph people or objects that affirm their identity or represent their important goals. Instructions for this variation read as follows:

> Throughout the course of the day today, you will take photographs of your everyday life. As you do this exercise, think about the things in your life that are *central to who you are*. If you wanted someone to understand you and what you most care about, how would you capture this? Although this is highly personal, some examples might include sports equipment, a memento from a favorite time spent with your romantic partner, or a textbook from your favorite class. Have your camera or camera phone handy and take at least five photographs of these things today. It is important to take the activity seriously and not rush through it.

This variation is effective because it encourages students to focus on what they value most in life, and it may have broader benefits. For example, research shows that students who engage in such self-affirmation through writing earn higher grades and experience less stress (Cohen, Garcia, Apfel, & Master, 2006; Creswell et al., 2005). Although the subject matter students choose for this version of the exercise might resemble the people or objects from the previous version that bring them happiness or joy, the motivation behind the photographs should differ. This variation is well suited to a discussion focusing on important life goals that promote the eudaimonic happiness associated with having meaning and purpose (see Chapter 4, this volume; cf. Kashdan, Biswas-Diener, & King, 2008).

An interpersonal component could also be added to a mindful photography exercise. For example, students could be asked to e-mail their photographs to friends or family members or to upload their photographs to a social networking site such as Facebook. This process provides students the additional benefit of receiving feedback on their photographs from others who may have a fresh perspective, perhaps helping to further counteract the adaptation process. That is, it can help make the things that a person has gotten used to fresh and exciting again. For example, an out-of-state friend may comment on something that the student has been taking for granted, such as the beauty of his snowy surroundings or the superiority of his neighborhood pizza parlor. Depending on class size and the amount of time the instructor wishes to devote, another variation may involve students presenting one or two of their favorite photographs to the class, with a brief explanation of what the photograph means to them. This adds another interpersonal component to the activity while promoting a positive classroom atmosphere.

Data on self-reported appreciation, positive emotions, happiness, and other outcomes of interest can easily be collected before and after the photography activity, so that instructors can determine whether mindful photography is leading to meaningful increases in positive outcomes. Short of these data, students should be eager to engage in discussion on the thoughts and feelings they experienced while taking the photographs, and, if applicable, while sharing or discussing them with others.

If instructors wish to test the effectiveness of variations of the mindful photography exercise, students could be randomly assigned to one of several photography conditions. Some could be instructed to take photographs of targets that lead them to experience happiness or joy versus targets that represent their valued goals, as described above, while others could be asked to take photographs without further instruction. Alternatively, students could be randomly assigned to take a different number of photographs (e.g., three, five, seven). In addition to serving as a demonstration for how to conduct, analyze, and interpret experimental studies, results from such class experiments can stimulate discussion on the most effective implementation strategies. Given the practically limitless memory capacity of digital cameras, some individuals could easily take this activity to the extreme. Others, by contrast, might feel inept at photography or become frustrated or burned out over the course of the assignment. Therefore, as is the case with all happiness-increasing strategies, it is important to question the extent to which this strategy is effective and to explore which variations are optimal.

DISCUSSION

According to Ansel Adams,

> Both the grand and the intimate aspects of nature can be revealed in the expressive photograph. Both can stir enduring affirmations and discoveries, and can surely help the spectator in his search for identification with the vast world of natural beauty and the wonder surrounding him. (Adams, 2012)

We believe that mindful photography is effective because it helps people to examine their everyday lives in a way that they normally do not—namely, through the lens of a camera, with an eye for beauty, meaning, and value. Preliminary data on the activity are promising, and students find it to be enjoyable. In the classroom, mindful photography will offer students firsthand experience with a novel mood-boosting activity and can give them a glimpse into the conduct of happiness-intervention studies. This activity should elicit discussion of the underlying processes involved in appreciation, savoring, and happiness.

WRITING COMPONENT

This activity can be easily adapted as a writing exercise. A general prompt might read as follows:

> After completing the photography exercise, reflect on the thoughts and feelings you had when (a) searching for appropriate subject matter, (b) taking the photographs, and (c) looking back at the photographs or sharing them with others (if applicable). Do you feel that it influenced your mood, emotions, and appreciation for things in your life? Why or why not? How long do you think the effects lasted? How could the activity be made more effective? Are there certain types of people who might benefit more or less from this activity? How sustainable are these changes? How can you ensure that the changes last?

This prompt encourages students to reflect on their personal experience with the activity while considering the psychological mechanisms underlying its benefits. It also encourages students to reflect on potential individual differences. To help encourage in-class discussion, students should complete the writing component before class.[1]

REFERENCES

Adams, A. (2012, April 12). Orchards of the Bay Area [Web log post]. Retrieved from http://www.anseladams.com/orchards-of-the-bay-area/

Bryant, F. B., Smart, C. M., & King, S. P. (2005). Using the past to enhance the present: Boosting happiness through positive reminiscence. *Journal of Happiness Studies, 6,* 227–260. doi:10.1007/s10902-005-3889-4

Cohen, G. L., Garcia, J., Apfel, N., & Master, A. (2006, September 1). Reducing the racial achievement gap: A social–psychological intervention. *Science, 313,* 1307–1310. doi:10.1126/science.1128317

Creswell, J. D., Welch, W., Taylor, S. E., Sherman, D. K., Gruenewald, T., & Mann, T. (2005). Affirmation of personal values buffers neuroendocrine and psychological stress responses. *Psychological Science, 16,* 846–851. doi:10.1111/j.1467-9280.2005.01624.x

Kashdan, T. B., Biswas-Diener, R., & King, L. A. (2008). Reconsidering happiness: The costs of distinguishing between hedonics and eudaimonia. *The Journal of Positive Psychology, 3,* 219–233. doi:10.1080/17439760802303044

Kurtz, J. L. (2011). *Seeing through new eyes: An experimental investigation of the benefits of mindful photography.* Unpublished manuscript, Department of Psychology, James Madison University, Harrisonburg, VA.

Lyubomirsky, S. (2008). *The how of happiness. A scientific approach to getting the life you want.* New York, NY: Penguin Press.

Lyubomirsky, S., Sheldon, K. M., & Schkade, D. (2005). Pursuing happiness: The architecture of sustainable change. *Review of General Psychology, 9,* 111–131. doi:10.1037/1089-2680.9.2.111

---

[1]To better grasp this topic, instructors and students are encouraged to consult the following source: Lyubomirsky (2008).

21

HOPE
HOPE PROJECTS TO ONE'S FUTURE SELF
Jeana L. Magyar-Moe

This activity affords students the opportunity to deepen their understanding of hope theory through the creation of hope projects regarding their future goals. Students will experience "hope reminding" when they receive their hope project via U.S. mail from their instructor after the course has ended.

CONCEPT

This activity is designed to help students apply hope theory to significant, long-term personal life goals to develop and sustain agency thinking (i.e., motivation). In addition, it will help students to develop pathways and consider alternative routes toward their goals over time as obstacles may arise. This activity entails the creation of verbal and pictorial representations of the three components of hope in relation to personal goal pursuits. The activity can be carried out in hard-copy or digital formats.

MATERIALS NEEDED

Each student will need one 9" × 12" envelope (or if sending a CD-ROM or USB drive, whatever envelope is appropriate), several postage stamps, and any craft materials necessary to create the project of choice (commonly used materials include digital camera and photo printer, card stock paper, glue).

INSTRUCTIONS

Hope is a positive psychological construct that can lead to the enhancement of positive emotions about the future (Snyder, 2000). Hope consists of one's perceptions regarding one's abilities to conceptualize goals clearly, develop specific strategies to reach those goals (pathways thinking), and find and maintain motivation for following through with those strategies (agency thinking; Snyder 1994). Both the pathways and agency components of hope are necessary, as neither alone is sufficient to sustain successful goal pursuits. According to hope theory, a goal can be anything that an individual desires to experience, create, get, do, or become. As such, a goal may be a significant, lifelong pursuit (e.g., creating and managing a successful small business), or it may be mundane and brief (e.g., completing weekly grocery shopping). Goals also may vary in terms of having perceived probabilities of attainment that range from very low to very high. Individuals with high hope prefer "stretch goals" that are slightly more difficult than previously attained goals (Lopez et al., 2004).

Students should be instructed to think about their goals for some specified window of time (e.g., the upcoming year). One can adjust the time frame of the goal setting based

---

[1]To better grasp this topic, instructors and students are encouraged to consult the following sources: Lopez, Ciarlelli, Coffman, Stone, and Wyatt (2000); Seligman (2002); Snyder, Rand, and Sigmon (2002); Snyder and Shorey (2002); and Snyder et al. (2002).

DOI: 10.1037/14042-022
Activities for Teaching Positive Psychology: A Guide for Instructors, J. J. Froh and A. C. Parks (Editors)

on what may be most logical for the students with which one is working. For example, freshmen might consider goals spanning their 4-year college careers. Alternatively, this activity can be designed to be completed during a single semester (spanning 3–4 months) such that student feedback can be obtained as part of the course. The worksheet in Appendix 21.1 can be used to help students develop and refine their goals such that they are challenging yet attainable. The worksheet also prompts students to develop pathways and agency thinking in relation to their major goal.

On completion of the worksheet, students should be instructed to create a physical representation of their goals, pathways, and agency plans in order to enhance goal visualization. The following example illustrates how this might be accomplished with photographs. A student whose goal is to get into medical school might create a medical school acceptance letter and have his or her photo taken holding the letter in hand. Next, the student would take photos that show the student engaging in strategies that will move him or her closer to the goal. Such photos represent pathways thinking. In this example, they might include pictures of the student as he or she is studying at the library, spending time in the chemistry laboratory, or attending meetings of the university premed student organization. Finally, the student would capture images that represent various sources of motivation toward his or her goal pursuits. For example, one might photograph his or her mentors, influential family members or friends, or other sources of motivation. Students should be invited to be creative and to produce projects that are meaningful to them. The only limitation is that each project should include some sort of narrative—captions to photos or PowerPoint slides, a written letter, or a story or poem that lays out their goals, pathways, and agency plans.

The hope project (either hard copy materials or the compact disc or flash drive that contains digital files) should be placed inside a self-addressed, stamped envelope to be mailed by the course instructor to the students on the specified future date. If students are uncertain about their future personal mailing addresses, they should be instructed to have their letters mailed to them via the address of a family member or friend who maintains a permanent residence. Instructors should insert a letter (see Appendix 21.2 for an example) into the envelopes containing the hope projects before sealing and eventually sending them to the students. The letter includes reminder information for the students regarding how to make sense of and utilize their hope projects on receipt of these materials at the future date.

DISCUSSION

Key to the success of this activity for fostering higher levels of hope within students is that it contain both hope-enhancing and hope-reminding components. *Hope-enhancing* strategies typically involve enlisting individuals in tasks that are designed to (a) conceptualize reasonable goals more clearly, (b) produce numerous pathways to attainment, (c) summon the energy to maintain goal pursuits, and (d) frame obstacles as challenges to be overcome. *Hope reminding* entails promotion of the deliberate use of hopeful cognitions via activities that prompt such thinking (Lopez et al., 2004).

Students should be encouraged to put a significant amount of time and energy into this activity to increase the likelihood of a meaningful outcome upon future receipt of their hope projects. To date, feedback from former students who completed this activity indicates that on receipt of their hope projects, they feel proud and energized regarding successful completion or continued progress toward their goal pursuits, which further enhances agency thinking. This response is exemplified in the following e-mail from a former positive psychology student:

> I felt compelled to contact you after receiving my hope letter in the mail this week. I wrote the letter five years ago in your positive psychology class. I had forgotten all about the letter and it was such a welcomed surprise! I had written the letter right after taking my GRE and was just beginning to look into graduate school for counseling education. The letter made me smile, remembering and reflecting on the fear and anticipation for the future. It is amazing how everything has a way of turning out. I vividly remember you encouraging us to "create" our own futures. I am grateful for that encouragement as nearly everything I hoped and wrote about in my letter has happened (outside of believing I would have three children by now!). I graduated with a master's degree in mental health counseling and I am currently accruing my hours toward my professional counseling license. Seeing how far I have come toward achieving the goals I had set for myself while still an undergraduate student has left me feeling happy and proud of myself. Very cool. Thank you for this assignment!

Alternatively, some students report feeling disappointed or shocked by how far they have strayed from their own goals. For these students, the hope project serves to either motivate them to recommit to their original goals or to take time to develop new goals based on current life circumstances. This response is exemplified in the following e-mail message from a former positive psychology student:

> Three months ago I got my hope letter in the mail that I wrote to myself two years ago when I was in the positive psychology class that you taught. At the time, I did not think the hope activity would really be meaningful or useful in my life—I was completely wrong! Since I wrote that hope letter, I had dropped out of college and was caught up in some activities that I am not very proud of. I was so far from the goals that I had set for myself just a few years ago that I could not fully comprehend it at first. Part of me wanted to just rip up and throw away my hope letter and to act as if I had never received it. Then I realized that this was exactly the wake-up call that I needed to make some important changes in my life. Long story short, as a result of seeing my own goals on paper and realizing how those goals were still very important to me, I left a very unhealthy relationship, started going to therapy, and am about to resume my junior year of college to finish my bachelor's degree!

Inclusion of Appendix 21.2 in the envelope with the student hope project is important, especially for those students who are not on track with their goals and are initially upset about this. The letter serves to help such students understand how to make constructive use of their hope project. Finally, be sure to have students write the date that the hope project is to be sent to them on the back of the envelope, keep the envelopes in a secure storage area, and develop a reminder system for ensuring that the hope projects are mailed in a timely fashion.

REFERENCES   Lopez, S. J., Ciarlelli, R., Coffman, L., Stone, M., & Wyatt, L. (2000). Diagnosing for strengths: On measuring hope building blocks. In C. R. Snyder (Ed.), *Handbook of hope: Theory, measures, and interventions* (pp. 57–85). San Diego, CA: Academic Press.

Lopez, S. J., Snyder, C. R., Magyar-Moe, J. L., Edwards, L. M., Pedrotti, J. T., Janowski, K., . . . Pressgrove, C. (2004). Strategies for accentuating hope. In P. A. Linley & S. Joseph (Eds.), *Positive psychology in practice* (pp. 388–404). Hoboken, NJ: Wiley.

Seligman, M. E. P. (2002). *Authentic happiness: Using the new positive psychology to realize your potential for lasting fulfillment.* New York, NY: Free Press.

Snyder, C. R. (1994). *The psychology of hope: You can get there from here.* New York, NY: Free Press.

Snyder, C. R. (2000). *Handbook of hope: Theory, measures, and applications.* San Diego, CA: Academic Press.

Snyder, C. R., Rand, K. L., & Sigmon, D. R. (2002). Hope theory: A member of the positive psychology family. In C. R. Snyder & S. J. Lopez (Eds.), *Handbook of positive psychology* (pp. 257–276). New York, NY: Oxford University Press.

Snyder, C. R., & Shorey, H. S. (2002). Hope in the classroom: The role of positive psychology in academic achievement and psychology curriculum. *Psychology Teacher Network, 12,* 1–9.

Snyder, C. R., Shorey, H. S., Cheavens, J., Pulvers, K. M., Adams, V. H., III, & Wiklund, C. (2002). Hope and academic success in college. *Journal of Educational Psychology, 94,* 820–826. doi:10.1037/0022-0663.94.4.820

Appendix 21.1

This worksheet has been designed to help you through the process of developing goals for the purpose of enhancing your levels of hope. To help you figure out where to begin in terms of creating goals for your life, please think about the major domains of life, as listed below, and then indicate which area or areas you would like to focus on when completing your hope project activity.

Life Domains

Home/family	Religion/spirituality
Work	Physical health
School	Civic engagement
Social relationships	Athletics
Romantic relationships	Arts/music
Hobbies	Other

Life Domain(s) Chosen:

_____

_____

_____

Next, on a separate piece of paper, state your goal(s) for this life domain or domains as specifically as you can and be sure to phrase your goals in positive terms.

Then, complete the following prompts regarding your goal(s):

1. The pathways I will need to follow to put this goal into action are . . .
2. I will find and sustain the motivation to work toward my goals by . . .
3. The challenges that I might face as I work toward my goals are . . .
4. I can navigate around those potential challenges by . . .

Important Reminders: Throughout the process of structuring your goals, remember to break large goals down into a series of smaller goals, and do not put too much pressure on yourself to accomplish large goals all at once. Also, if your plan for reaching a goal fails, do not get down on yourself or give up. Rather, learn from it and create an alternative plan for reaching your goal. If your goal is truly blocked, find a substitute goal to focus on. As you work toward your goals, be sure to enjoy the process and be kind to yourself. Talk to yourself in positive terms and remind yourself of your past goal successes, especially if you find yourself losing motivation (Lopez et al., 2004).

Appendix 21.2

Dear Former Positive Psychology Student,

Please find enclosed your hope project completed during the _____(term) of _____ (year). In reviewing your project, please be sure to reflect on your goal pursuits and consider all factors that have either allowed you to accomplish or maintain progress toward your goals or have blocked your goal efforts.

If you have successfully completed your goals or remain on track toward your goal pursuits, take a moment to celebrate this success and to consider developing new goals, pathways, and agency thinking for the year(s) ahead.

If you have not made progress on your goal pursuits, take a moment to consider what caused this to happen. There are many possibilities, including obstacles that felt too difficult to overcome, lack of motivation, inability to generate alternative pathways, or a conscious decision to change goal pursuits. No matter what the reason, if your plan for reaching your goals did not work, please, do not get down on yourself or give up! Rather, learn from it and create an alternative plan for reaching your goal now that you have better insight into the task at hand. If your goal is truly blocked, find a substitute goal to focus on.

As you work toward your goals, be sure to enjoy the process and be kind to yourself. Talk to yourself in positive terms and remind yourself of your past goal successes, especially if you find yourself losing motivation.

If you are so inclined, I would love to hear from you. Please e-mail me at _____ to update me on how you are doing and to provide me with information related to your reaction to receiving your hope project.

Sincerely,

_____

22 MATERIALISM
A TEACHING TOOL FOR DISENGAGING FROM MATERIALISM: THE COMMERCIAL MEDIA FAST

Yuna L. Ferguson and Tim Kasser

In this activity, students are challenged to avoid exposure to all forms of commercial media in their lives for several days. By doing so, students learn about the pervasiveness of commercial media in their everyday activities (e.g., e-mailing, eating at restaurants, socializing with friends) and are encouraged to reflect on how consumer culture may encourage them to pursue the materialistic aspirations known to be associated with a lower level of well-being.

CONCEPT

This activity demonstrates the extent to which students' lives are saturated with commercial media from corporations and businesses that encourage the purchase of products and services. Because exposure to commercial messages is among the causes of a strong focus on materialistic aspirations and goals (Kasser, Ryan, Couchman, & Sheldon, 2004), abstaining from commercial media for several days may help students gain insight into how this important feature of contemporary culture promotes the materialistic values (and behaviors) that are known to be associated with lower well-being (Kasser et al., 2004). This activity may also serve as practice for students who decide to limit their exposure to commercial media in the future.

MATERIALS NEEDED

This activity does not require any additional materials apart from the suggested readings.

INSTRUCTIONS

From the moment of waking up in the morning to the moment of falling asleep, the typical American is exposed to an enormous number of advertising messages, with estimates ranging from 3,600 to 5,000 ads per day (Jhally, 1997; Story, 2007). Commercial media (i.e., advertising that is intended to increase profit for some private entity) are present on television, in newspapers, and in magazines and reach the public through the Internet on popular social networking websites such as Facebook and major e-mail account sites such as Gmail. Websites popular among college students that offer free services, such as the music site Pandora.com and the video site YouTube.com, also sell advertising space to for-profit corporations. Even when people go to the movies or a sporting event, they are exposed to advertising before the event or during intermissions.

Although many students agree that commercial media abound in their social surroundings, they may be unaware of the almost inescapable presence in their everyday activities. Having grown up in a culture saturated with marketing and advertising, perhaps they have become desensitized to its presence. Encouraging students to actively

DOI: 10.1037/14042-023
Activities for Teaching Positive Psychology: A Guide for Instructors, J. J. Froh and A. C. Parks (Editors)

and systematically evaluate both their activities and their social surroundings for the presence of commercial media may help them understand the extent to which commercial media permeate their lives. In the commercial media fast activity, students are asked to abstain from all forms of commercial media for a period of time, at least for a few days. Doing so requires them first to scrutinize all activities in which they engage and then to (try to) avoid those that involve exposure to commercial media. In our previous use of this exercise, students have abstained from activities such as watching television and listening to commercial radio, as well as using Facebook, going to the movies, and even wearing clothing with logos of profit-driven entities. Students may also be exposed to commercial media in their social activities with friends and in activities required in classes; as such, this exercise may also lead to reflection on the extent to which commercial media are part of their interpersonal and academic lives.

The commercial media fast may differ from most other activities suggested by positive psychologists in that it does not purport to increase well-being directly; in fact, many students may find their media fast to be an uncomfortable experience, not unlike trying to quit smoking. Instead, we believe that this experience helps students to understand their place in consumer culture, to reflect on how consumer culture may encourage them to pursue the materialistic aspirations known to be associated with lower well-being, and to empower their decision to limit their exposure to commercial media, if they so choose. Furthermore, although this activity may not directly influence students' well-being, our pilot study suggests that many students find that it has other positive consequences. For instance, students have commented that they have had more time to complete coursework, to sleep, to engage in creative leisure activities, and to carry on meaningful conversations with their friends (about consumer culture and other topics). These are the very kinds of activities associated with the intrinsic values and goals known to promote higher levels of well-being (Kasser & Ryan, 1996). Thus, if students voluntarily extend their fast, they may come to focus on these positive alternative activities habitually, which may then lead to greater sustained well-being.

PROCEDURE

Before students are assigned the commercial media fast, they might find it beneficial to read and discuss research about materialistic goals and well-being, as doing so may provide more context and purpose for this activity. Research differentiates two types of goals that are particularly relevant for well-being (Kasser & Ryan, 1996). On the one hand, there are the *intrinsic* goals for aims such as helping the community, growing as a person, and having close interpersonal relationships; these goals are known to promote higher levels of well-being. On the other hand, there are the *extrinsic* goals, which include popularity, wealth, and appearance; a strong focus on these goals is consistently associated with lower levels of well-being. The distinctions between these goals and their correlates with well-being have been replicated in numerous studies and in various nations around the world. Correlational studies have shown that a higher level of well-being is enjoyed by those who have a preference for intrinsic versus extrinsic aspirations (Kasser & Ryan, 1993; Sheldon, Ryan, Deci, & Kasser, 2004), not only among Americans but also among Germans (Schmuck, Kasser, & Ryan, 2000) and Russians (Ryan et al., 1999). Furthermore, individuals who pursue intrinsic goals report a greater positive change in well-being over a period of a year (Sheldon et al., 2004).

A particularly important point for students to grasp is that one of the known causes of a relatively strong focus on the materialistic, extrinsic values is exposure to social models that encourage such aims in life (Kasser et al., 2004), including commercial media. Commercial media typically glorify materialistic lifestyles that incorporate extrinsic concerns, as advertisements typically tell people that to be happy, they need the right kind of portable music player, an expensive automobile, and fashionable clothing, among many other products and services. These ads often tie their products symbolically to extrinsic values, which may then lead individuals who see the ads to define their identities increasingly around consumerism, wealth, and possessions (Wright, Claiborne, & Sirgy, 1992). For example, an individual who purchases the latest and most popular portable music player or the luxury brand handbag may expect these items' popularity to rub off on her, resulting in a perceived elevation of her social image (Banerjee & Dittmar, 2008). However, as the research shows, prioritizing materialistic messages and "buying into" the advertising messages that consumption brings happiness often backfire. Furthermore, because materialistic, extrinsic goals tend to stand in a dynamic tension with intrinsic goals (Grouzet et al., 2005), a relatively strong focus on them can "crowd out" the extent to which individuals focus on the more satisfying aims of having good relationships, pursuing their own interests, and contributing to the world around them.

The commercial media fast helps students gain an awareness of the many for-profit entities attempting to influence their behavior, thoughts, feelings, and values. In the learning activity we piloted, students were asked to try to exclude from their lives all commercial media. We defined *commercial media* as including messages in any form that attempted to sell a particular product or service to garner profit for the seller or to foster a positive perception of the profit-driven entity. Based on this definition, watching most television and listening to most radio would need to be avoided, as both forms of media are largely supported by advertising; however, certain forms of TV and radio, such as PBS and NPR, may be commercial-free (excluding messages of corporate support). After the instructor has raised these obvious instances, it may be useful to facilitate a class discussion about other media outlets that students should avoid to complete the assignment successfully. Students will likely begin to recognize, for example, that many e-mail accounts, such as Gmail or Hotmail, host commercial media, as do their Facebook pages and many other websites. Students may even need to examine the clothes they wear so that they cease being "walking advertisements." We have also found it useful to incorporate the notion of "relapse prevention" into the assignment, letting students know that if and when they fall back into their previous commercial media habits during the duration of the assignment, they should acknowledge the relapse, forgive themselves, and return to their fast.

After completion of the activity, we suggest that the instructor ask the students to write a paper reflecting on their experiences (see the Writing Component section). We found that doing so provided excellent material for class discussion once the assignment was completed.

DISCUSSION Based on a pilot study ($N = 15$), we found that this activity enhanced students' awareness of the amount of media they typically consume ($M = 5.87$, $SD = .92$ on a scale of $1 = not\ at\ all$ to $7 = to\ a\ great\ extent$). While we had been worried that students might feel somewhat overwhelmed by their increased awareness of the extent to which commercial media are present in their lives, we found that after the assignment students reported that they felt slightly more in control over their consumption of commercial media ($M = 4.87$, $SD = 1.51$ on a scale of $1 = much\ less\ control$ to $7 = much\ more\ control$).

Because, as these students quickly discovered, ads are almost everywhere in our surroundings and daily activities, this commercial media fast was somewhat difficult to complete for many students ($M = 4.30$, $SD = 1.25$ on a scale of $1 = $ *not at all difficult* to $7 = $ *extremely difficult*). However, the difficulty of abstaining completely may be an important lesson in itself; as one student stated, "This project is probably impossible for anyone today to complete honestly without cheating, and therefore it makes a great point about the current culture of consumption." As expected, our students also noted that completing this activity disrupted many typical social activities, such as watching online videos with their friends or getting updates about their friends through Facebook; class discussion can be facilitated about how commercial media have made inroads into students' social relationships. Many of our pilot students also noted that as a result of temporarily giving up certain activities associated with media, they found more time to sleep and focus on their homework. What's more, some students reported that during the commercial media fast, they engaged in more activities relevant to intrinsic goals, including pursuing creative activities, such as playing music, and spending more time talking with others face-to-face. One student commented, "Media promotes the idea that we will be more connected and happier if we spend more time interacting with it. . . . I found the opposite experience. I consumed less media and [had] more personal experiences."

Our pilot students were all enrolled in a course on alternatives to consumerism, and therefore these students may be more inclined to engage in such an activity or might find it more valuable compared with other students. To the extent that students are willing to engage in such an activity that requires them to drastically alter their everyday activities, the pilot study suggested that they may find it challenging but beneficial. One student summed up his experience by stating that, "There is much to be said for facing your fears and overcoming them. That is what I'm trying to do. I don't want to feel hopeless and so I'm making a conscious effort to increase my sense of agency." Although the students in this activity fasted for only 1 week, we think that the beneficial outcomes of the activity may increase if students are instructed to fast for a longer period of time, as they may increasingly orient their lives away from the activities associated with extrinsic goals that are encouraged by commercial media, and instead organize their lives around experiences more supportive of the pursuit of intrinsic goals.

WRITING COMPONENT

To encourage students to reflect deeply on their experience, we suggest assigning a response paper that asks them to answer the following questions. This paper can be written before or during class, so that students are better prepared to discuss their experiences with classmates in small groups of three to five. The instructor may then help students summarize their activity experience by asking the groups to share the main points of their discussions. We asked our students to write about and then discuss the following types of questions:

1. What were your initial expectations about the activity? How did you think you would react to it?
2. How did you plan the fast?
3. What did you experience during the commercial media fast? What difficulties did you encounter in undergoing the fast?
4. How did other people react to your attempt to engage in the fast?

5. How did this project change your understanding of your place in consumer culture?

6. How do you think your life might be different if advertising for products and services did not exist or existed at a very limited level?[1]

REFERENCES

Adbusters. (n.d.). *Spoof ads*. Retrieved from http://www.adbusters.org/spoofads

Banerjee, R., & Dittmar, H. (2008). Individual differences in children's materialism: The role of peer relations. *Personality and Social Psychology Bulletin, 34,* 17–31. doi:10.1177/0146167207309196

Grouzet, F. M. E., Kasser, T., Ahuvia, A., Fernandez-Dols, J. M., Kim, Y., Lau, S., . . . Sheldon, K. M. (2005). The structure of goal contents across 15 cultures. *Journal of Personality and Social Psychology, 89,* 800–816. doi:10.1037/0022-3514.89.5.800

Jhally, S. (Producer, Writer, & Director). (1997). *Advertising and the end of the world* (Documentary film). Amherst, MA: Media Education Foundation.

Kasser, T., & Ryan, R. M. (1993). A dark side of the American dream: Correlates of financial success as a central life aspiration. *Journal of Personality and Social Psychology, 65,* 410–422. doi:10.1037/0022-3514.65.2.410

Kasser, T., & Ryan, R. M. (1996). Further examining the American dream: Differential correlates of intrinsic and extrinsic goals. *Personality and Social Psychology Bulletin, 22,* 280–287. doi:10.1177/0146167296223006

Kasser, T., Ryan, R. M., Couchman, C. E., & Sheldon, K. M. (2004). Materialistic values: Their causes and consequences. In T. Kasser & A. D. Kanner (Eds.), *Psychology and consumer culture: The struggle for a good life in a materialistic world* (pp. 11–28). Washington, DC: American Psychological Association. doi:10.1037/10658-002

Ryan, R. M., Chirkov, V. I., Little, T. D., Sheldon, K. M., Timoshina, E., & Deci, E. L. (1999). The American dream in Russia: Extrinsic aspirations and well-being in two cultures. *Personality and Social Psychology Bulletin, 25,* 1509–1524. doi:10.1177/01461672992510007

Schmuck, P., Kasser, T., & Ryan, R. M. (2000). Intrinsic and extrinsic goals: Their structure and relationship to well-being in German and U.S. college students. *Social Indicators Research, 50,* 225–241. doi:10.1023/A:1007084005278

Sheldon, K. M., Ryan, R. M., Deci, E. L., & Kasser, T. (2004). The independent effects of goal contents and motives on well-being: It's both what you pursue and why you pursue it. *Personality and Social Psychology Bulletin, 30,* 475–486. doi:10.1177/0146167203261883

Story, L. (2007, January 15). Anywhere the eye can see, it's likely to see an ad. *The New York Times*. Retrieved from http://www.nytimes.com/2007/01/15/business/media/15everywhere.html?_r=2&pagewan ted=1

Wright, N. D., Claiborne, C. B., & Sirgy, M. J. (1992). The effects of product symbolism on consumer self-concept. *Advances in Consumer Research. Association for Consumer Research, 19,* 311–318.

---

[1]To better grasp this topic, instructors and students are encouraged to consult the following sources: Adbusters (n.d.); Jhally (1997); and Kasser et al. (2004).

23 SAVORING
THE SAVORING EXPEDITION:
AN EXERCISE TO CULTIVATE SAVORING

Patrick R. Harrison, Jennifer L. Smith, and Fred B. Bryant

This activity encourages students who have already been introduced to savoring in their positive psychology class to apply what they have learned. Students will have the opportunity to practice their savoring skills by identifying and seeking out a positive experience, savoring it, and reflecting on the strategies they used to savor that experience.

CONCEPT

Have you ever been engaged in a positive experience and become aware, while it was happening, that you were having "the time of your life"? Have you ever enjoyed a positive activity so much that you wished it could go on forever? Are there things that you think or do during especially happy moments that intensify your positive feelings or make them last longer? Thoughts and behaviors that regulate good feelings in response to positive events are known as *savoring strategies* (Bryant & Veroff, 2007). Unfortunately, we often fail to appreciate these experiences fully, and we may not be consciously aware of the specific things that make these experiences enjoyable. This activity is about becoming more aware of how to savor positive experiences.

MATERIALS NEEDED

Students will need some free time, comfortable clothes, and an open mind. They will also need to be relatively free from worries, distractions, and time pressure.

INSTRUCTIONS

The savoring expedition is broken down into three phases, each involving several simple steps. The steps are designed to provide guidance for getting started, but students may deviate from these instructions if they feel it will help them savor more fully. The guidelines that follow should be copied and presented to students (see Appendix 23.1 for a sample handout that describes these steps in shorthand).

Phase 1: Plan Your Savoring Expedition

    Step 1: Choose Something Enjoyable to Savor. There are many types of positive experiences that people find enjoyable or worth savoring. For example, some people

---

This exercise is dedicated to the memory of Charles W. Harrison—a man who showed others the joys of savoring each and every day.

DOI: 10.1037/14042-024
Activities for Teaching Positive Psychology: A Guide for Instructors, J. J. Froh and A. C. Parks (Editors)
Copyright © 2013 by the American Psychological Association. All rights reserved.

enjoy going to an art museum, a movie, or a nightclub, whereas others like to go for walks on the beach. In other cases, individuals prefer to go to places that have special meaning or memories for them (e.g., a park or playground that they like, or a summer camp they attended as a child). Before embarking on your savoring expedition, think about an activity, experience, place, or object that you find enjoyable. This will be the target of your expedition.

Step 2: Set Aside Some Time for Savoring. Once you have identified an activity, experience, place, or object that you could savor, set aside some time. Try to find a time when you are free from having to think about other things or engage in other activities.

Step 3: Gather Materials for Your Savoring Expedition. Because lacking important necessities can interfere with the quality of your savoring expedition, take time beforehand to determine the things (e.g., money, comfortable shoes) you will need to have with you on your expedition.

Phase 2: Embark on Your Savoring Expedition

Step 4: Set Out on Your Savoring Expedition. When the day and time arrive, set out on your savoring expedition. When you arrive at your destination, try to set aside worries or concerns that might limit your ability to savor. Ty to be fully in the moment and appreciate what is immediately in front of you.

Step 5: Savor. Try to pinpoint what you find enjoyable about the particular activity, experience, place, or object you've chosen. For example, you might notice the sights, sounds, and smells around you as you acknowledge the beauty of the situation. You might also think about the emotions you feel and the thoughts that cross your mind. If you find that you are having trouble savoring, do not criticize or force yourself. Some people find savoring more difficult than others, and the ability to savor will depend, in large part, on your level of comfort with the situation. If you feel your savoring expedition is too contrived or unnatural, then go home and try again another time.

Step 6: Document Your Experiences. Identify the specific things that make the expedition enjoyable, interesting, or worthwhile. Try to describe what you feel by naming the specific positive feelings (e.g., happiness, joy, contentment, peace) you experience. Identifying exactly what you are feeling will help you build a richer memory of the savoring experience and help you remember and relive it more vividly later.

Phase 3: Reflect on Your Savoring Expedition

Step 7: Revisit Your Expedition. After you return home from your savoring expedition, look back on your experiences. Try to remember the sights, sounds, and smells. Think about the emotions and thoughts you experienced. Carefully reflect on what you enjoyed about the activity, experience, location, or object you chose to savor.

Step 8: Recount Your Expedition to Others. Sometimes, the joy in savoring occurs even more intensely after your time with that activity, experience, place, or object is over. If you have the desire, tell someone else about the activity, experience, place, or object you savored on your expedition. If you are comfortable doing so, write a narrative account of your experiences and consider how you might find ways to savor more fully in your everyday life.

DISCUSSION

Psychology has traditionally focused on understanding how individuals cope with negative life events. However, psychological well-being is also a function of people's capacity to savor, or to derive and manage positive feelings in response to positive experiences (Bryant & Veroff, 2007). This exercise was designed to encourage proactive, mindful savoring by having students take a savoring expedition. Although the word *expedition* implies an active pursuit of some goal, expeditions can also be exploratory. In this case, students were encouraged to explore how they might deliberately promote savoring in their own life. Because what works for one person might not work for another, this exercise was designed to be flexible. When students finish, they should be able to identify what cognitive and behavioral strategies helped them savor more regularly and mindfully.

After returning from the savoring expedition, students should be encouraged to engage in a small group (three to four students) or class discussion about their experiences. Discuss the definition of savoring and determine whether students were able to become more mindful of opportunities to savor in their lives. Some individuals find savoring easier than others, so students should not be discouraged if they found this exercise difficult. As with almost any process, savoring may require practice, so encourage students to share strategies and approaches that worked for them. Discuss the lessons students learned about savoring in particular and positive psychology in general. Encourage students to go on another savoring expedition using the lessons they have learned from this one. In addition, if they feel comfortable doing so, encourage students to go on a savoring expedition in groups. The presence of others may boost the savoring experience for some.

WRITING COMPONENT

Before discussing their experiences, have students write responses to the following questions as a take-home assignment. While in small groups, have students discuss their answers to these questions:

1. How easy was it to savor the experiences you had while on your savoring expedition?
2. What strategies (e.g., thoughts or behaviors) did you use to get the most out of your savoring expedition?
3. What obstacles or impediments did you face that interfered with your ability to savor during your expedition?
4. How was your experience during the savoring expedition different from how you might normally have acted in the same situation?
5. How easy was it for you to relive your savoring expedition after it was over?
6. What advice would you give someone interested in try to enhance his or her ability to savor?
7. Why do we not savor more often or more fully during our everyday life? Are there ways to increase savoring in our daily life?
8. What have you learned from this exercise that you did not know beforehand?

Individuals may use a variety of savoring strategies to get the most out of positive experiences. The above questions are designed to encourage students to think about what types of savoring strategies work for them. Understanding these individual savoring strategies may help students integrate savoring into their everyday lives more effectively.[1]

REFERENCES

Bryant, F. B. (2003). Savoring Beliefs Inventory (SBI): A scale for measuring beliefs about savoring. *Journal of Mental Health, 12*, 175–196. doi:10.1080/0963823031000103489

Bryant, F. B., Chadwick, E. D., & Kluwe, K. (2011). Understanding the processes that regulate positive emotional experience: Unsolved problems and future directions for theory and research on savoring. *International Journal of Wellbeing, 1*, 107–126. doi:10.5502/ijw.v1i1.18

Bryant, F. B., Smart, C. M., & King, S. P. (2005). Using the past to enhance the present: Boosting happiness through positive reminiscence. *Journal of Happiness Studies, 6*, 227–260. doi:10.1007/s10902-005-3889-4

Bryant, F. B., & Veroff, J. (2007). *Savoring: A new model of positive experience.* Mahwah, NJ: Erlbaum.

Linley, A. P., & Joseph, S. (Eds.). (2004). *Positive psychology in practice.* Hoboken, NJ: Wiley.

Synder, C. R., & Lopez, S. J. (Eds.). (2005). *Handbook of positive psychology.* New York, NY: Oxford University Press.

---

[1]To better grasp this topic, instructors and students are encouraged to consult the following sources: Bryant (2003); Bryant, Chadwick, & Kluwe (2011); Bryant, Smart, & King (2005); Linley & Joseph (2004); Synder & Lopez (2005).

Appendix 23.1

Phase 1: Plan Your Savoring Expedition

    Step 1: Choose something to savor. Before embarking on your savoring expedition, think about an activity, experience, place, or object that you find enjoyable that will be the target of your expedition.

    Step 2: Set aside some time for savoring. Block out a time when you are free from having to think about other things or engage in other activities to savor.

    Step 3: Gather materials for your savoring expedition. Determine the things (e.g., money, comfortable shoes) you will need to have with you on your expedition.

Phase 2: Embark on Your Savoring Expedition

    Step 4: Set out on your savoring expedition. Try to be fully in the moment and appreciate what is immediately in front of you.

    Step 5: Savor. Try to pinpoint what you find enjoyable about the particular activity, experience, place, or object you are trying to savor.

    Step 6: Document your experiences. Identify the specific things that make the expedition enjoyable, interesting, or worthwhile.

Phase 3: Reflect on Your Savoring Expedition

    Step 7: Revisit your expedition. Carefully reflect on what you enjoyed about the activity, experience, location, or object you chose to savor.

    Step 8: Recount your expedition to others. If you have the desire, tell someone else about the activity, experience, place, or object you savored on your expedition. You may even want to write a narrative account of your experiences and consider how you might find ways to savor more fully in your everyday life.

24 MOTIVATION
INTERNALIZED MOTIVATION IN THE CLASSROOM
Kennon M. Sheldon

The motivation that students bring to a classroom setting is critical in determining how much, and how well, they learn. This activity allows students to assess and reflect on the quality of their own motivation for taking this particular class. In the process, important concepts from Deci and Ryan's self-determination theory are introduced.

CONCEPT
Self-determination theory research has demonstrated the importance of having *internalized motivation:* doing X because it is interesting and enjoyable or at least an expression of one's values and identity rather than doing X because one feels controlled by internal or external forces. This activity allows students to assess their own motivation for doing well in this class and to consider why their motivation may be suboptimal.

MATERIALS NEEDED
Each student will need a hard copy of a single-page motivation questionnaire (see Appendix 24.1).

INSTRUCTIONS
This can be a good activity for the first day of class because it invites reflection on why the student is taking the class and what, therefore, he or she might expect to get out of it. Such reflection may help the student to get more out of the class. This activity also invites more general reflection on the nature of the student's motivation in the world, and it can serve to illuminate recurring motivational problems and potential solutions.

Hand out the questionnaire (see Appendix 24.1) and prompt students as follows:

> Think about why you are trying to do well in this class. Then, rate each of the possible reasons, below. Of course, people can do things for more than one reason, so you might give high ratings to more than one of the questions.

Give them a couple of minutes to make the five ratings.

Afterward, provide a short introduction to Deci and Ryan's self-determination theory (SDT; Deci & Ryan, 2000; Ryan & Deci, 2000, 2008). The theory is complex and multifaceted, and the five reasons provide a good entry point into it. In brief, SDT is a theory of optimal motivation, which begins with the concept of *intrinsic motivation.* This means doing something primarily because of the interest and enjoyment that activity provides (e.g., playing basketball, playing a video game, spending time with

DOI: 10.1037/14042-025

Activities for Teaching Positive Psychology: A Guide for Instructors, J. J. Froh and A. C. Parks (Editors)

friends). When the concept of intrinsic motivation was proposed in the early 1970s, it was a somewhat radical idea because the then-dominant behaviorist and drive theory perspectives view behavior as motivated by expected rewards and reinforcements or by the need to assuage biological demands. However, the intrinsic motivation concept fits well with the "cognitive revolution" and the idea that cognitive development is in large part internally driven via exploratory behavior.

Early research by Deci demonstrated the *undermining effect,* in which intrinsic motivation could be spoiled by rewards, competitions, deadlines, and social pressures. For example, research participants who were paid to solve previously enjoyable puzzles did not want to play with them when left alone during a "free choice" period. This is the opposite of what the behaviorist reinforcement perspective predicts. Does undermining matter? Yes, because intrinsically motivated people try harder and longer, perform more flexibly and creatively, and learn more deeply than extrinsically motivated people (see Ryan & Deci, 2008, for a recent review).

Later, SDT evolved to incorporate other forms of motivation besides intrinsic and extrinsic motivation (Ryan & Deci, 2000, 2008). This was necessary because not all important behaviors (e.g., changing diapers, filling out tax forms) can be fun and enjoyable. In these cases, it is beneficial if one can at least internalize the behaviors, so that one does them willingly, even if they are not enjoyable. Currently, SDT specifies not just one but three forms of extrinsic motivation, which vary in their degree of internalization. *External motivation* is based on expected rewards or avoided punishments and fits the tenets of behaviorist (operant) theory. When external motivation is dominant, there is no internalization of the behavior; it does not feel as if it emanates from or is endorsed by one's self. *Introjected motivation* is next on the internalization continuum. Here, there is partial internalization in that one part of the person is compelling another part of the person to act, usually to avoid guilt or bad feelings about oneself. Introjected motivation is a common target of psychodynamic therapy and fits the Freudian notion of the superego, which compels the person to do socially prescribed behavior. *Identified motivation* is next on the internalization continuum. Here, the nonintrinsically motivated behavior has been completely internalized; there is no internal resistance, and there is a willingness to do the behavior because it is important and valuable to the self, even when it is not enjoyable. Identified motivation fits the tenets of existential therapy and the idea that one should take full responsibility for one's choices rather than behaving in "bad faith."

It is also worth discussing *amotivation,* which according to SDT represents a sense of acting without having a clear intention of doing so—acting without knowing why or acting with a feeling of helplessness. In this view, an amotivated person is not a person who does nothing; instead, he or she acts, but with a feeling of passivity and without a clear intention.

Figure 24.1 presents a diagram containing the five forms of motivation, which could be used to help explain SDT to the students (Ryan & Deci, 2000). As can be seen, the motivations are viewed as lying on an *internalization continuum,* from not at all internalized into the self (amotivation and external motivation) to partially internalized (introjected motivation) to fully internalized (identified motivation) to automatically internalized (intrinsic motivation). The diagram also contrasts the three forms of extrinsic motivation (external, introjected, and identified) with intrinsic motivation. In addition, *autonomous* motivation (identified and intrinsic motivation) is con-

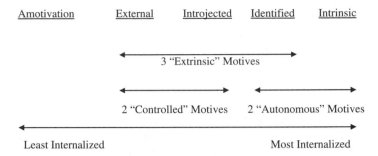

Amotivation   External   Introjected   Identified   Intrinsic

3 "Extrinsic" Motives

2 "Controlled" Motives   2 "Autonomous" Motives

Least Internalized   Most Internalized

Figure 24.1. *The motivation continuum. Adapted from "Self-Determination Theory and the Facilitation of Intrinsic Motivation, Social Development, and Well-Being," by R. M. Ryan and E. L. Deci, 2000, American Psychologist, 55, p. 72. Copyright 2000 by the American Psychological Association.*

trasted with *controlled* motivation (external and introjected motivation). Considering these concepts highlights the importance of identified motivation: Although it is not intrinsic (and thus, like diaper changing, is no fun), it can nevertheless still be autonomous and volitional because one stands behind the values and purposes expressed by the behavior (keeping one's baby healthy). Indeed, considerable research suggests that psychological maturity involves transmuting controlled motivations into autonomous ones; as people age, they tend to become more autonomous and less controlled in what they do, fitting the existentialist dictum to "grow up and take responsibility for one's actions" (Sheldon & Kasser, 2001).

Students' responses to the five questions can be handled in a number of ways. First, Question 5 in the handout assesses intrinsic motivation, and Question 2 assesses external motivation. Typically these ratings are negatively correlated, consistent with the undermining effect. Students might be prompted to think about why their external motivation is stronger than their intrinsic motivation (if this is the case) and to think about how they could enhance their intrinsic and reduce their external motivation. They could also be asked whether they agree that these two motivations conflict with each other. In addition, they could evaluate the extent to which that they feel amotivated, that is, the degree to which they do not know why they are in the class and do not expect to do at all well in the class. Amotivation is likely to be low in a positive psychology class, but students may be able to identify other classes that induce a sense of amotivation.

In line with typical research practice, students could also compute a *relative autonomy* score for their classroom motivation by adding the ratings for Questions 4 and 5 (identified and intrinsic) and then subtracting their ratings for Questions 2 and 3 (external and introjected). A relative autonomy score less than 0 suggests that the student has primarily controlled motivation, which is likely to impair his or her potential enjoyment of the class and ability to learn the material in a deep way. It may also reflect a maladaptive and disempowering way of "copping out" on one's chosen behaviors, that is, of not fully committing to something one has decided to do. A relative autonomy score greater than 0 suggests that the student's motivation is reasonably adaptive and optimal. The higher the positive score, the better. Thus, the combination of "5" ratings on identified (Question 4) and intrinsic (Question 5) and "1" ratings on external (Question 2) and introjected (Question 3) would be optimal. Of course, it is hard to deny that extrinsic motivations will always play a role; grades do matter, and guilt can be a powerful motivator. Still, the question suggested by SDT research is, How can these extrinsic motivators be minimized and downplayed, or even transmuted into identified motivation, the most adaptive form of extrinsic motivation?

DISCUSSION

There are many other potential avenues of discussion. Students could be prompted to compare this class with another for which they have a different quality of motivation. Why does this difference exist? Is it due to social pressures or stresses that may have undermined motivation in one type of class but not in another? What types of teacher, teaching style, or classroom process style are most conducive to promoting intrinsic motivation, and what types tend to undermine intrinsic motivation?

Students could also be prompted to consider their motivational style in general. Are they typically too passive or reward focused in life, or do they typically motivate themselves with guilt? Can they see how the latter motivational strategies may backfire, undermining their inherent exploratory urges? They might also think about changes in their own motivation over time. When they were younger, they might have cleaned up their room only because parents insisted; now, do they clean their living space for more internalized (self-endorsed) reasons? In other words, can they see a developmental progression in themselves from left to right on the internalization continuum? If so, can they imagine this happening with respect to their current "controlled" motivations?

WRITING COMPONENT

There are a wide variety of writing possibilities. Students could be asked to write about and explain their ratings on the five questions. Why did they make each rating, and do they agree that these ratings have the meaning claimed by SDT? They could also do a developmental analysis of their own academic motivation. What was their motivation like on their first day of school or in grade school? What has changed since then and why? Students could also construct a plan for enhancing their own level of academic internalization (if not for this positive psychology course, perhaps for some other less positive course!). What negative patterns of thought or motivation might they try to notice, challenge, and change? What affirmations or restatements can they make to remind themselves that this is what they have chosen to do and to convince themselves that it is important? If they cannot convince themselves of this, should they consider making a change (e.g., from premed major to dance major or psychology major to nursing major)?[1]

REFERENCES

Deci, E. L., & Ryan, R. M. (1985). *Intrinsic motivation and self-determination in human behavior.* New York, NY: Plenum.

Deci, E. L., & Ryan, R. M. (2000). The "what" and "why" of goal pursuits: Human needs and the self-determination of behavior. *Psychological Inquiry, 11,* 227–268. doi:10.1207/S15327965PLI1104_01

Ryan, R. M., & Connell, J. P. (1989). Perceived locus of causality and internalization: Examining reasons for acting in two domains. *Journal of Personality and Social Psychology, 57,* 749–761. doi:10.1037/0022-3514.57.5.749

---

[1]To better grasp this topic, instructors and students are encouraged to consult the following sources: Deci and Ryan (1985); Ryan and Connell (1989); Sheldon (2004); and Sheldon, Kashdan, and Steger (2011).

Ryan, R. M., & Deci, E. L. (2000). Self-determination theory and the facilitation of intrinsic motivation, social development, and well-being. *American Psychologist, 55,* 68–78. doi:10.1037/0003-066X.55.1.68

Ryan, R. M., & Deci, E. L. (2008). Self-determination theory and the role of basic psychological needs in personality and the organization of behavior. In O. John, R. Roberts, & L. A. Pervin (Eds.), *Handbook of personality: Theory and research* (pp. 654–678). New York, NY: Guilford.

Sheldon, K. M. (2004). *Optimal human being: An integrated multi-level perspective.* Mahwah, NJ: Erlbaum.

Sheldon, K. M., & Kasser, T. (2001). Getting older, getting better? Personal strivings and personality development across the life-course. *Developmental Psychology, 37,* 491–501. doi:10.1037/0012-1649.37.4.491

Sheldon, K. M., Kashdan, T., & Steger, M. (Eds.). (2011). *Designing the future of positive psychology: Taking stock and moving forward.* New York, NY: Oxford University Press.

Appendix 24.1

"What Is My Motivation?"

ASSIGNMENT RATING SHEET

Past research suggests that people may be motivated to do something for many different reasons. In this task, rate the following reasons for *why you want to do well in this class.* Of course, people can have more than one reason for doing something, so you might give more than one high rating. Use this scale:

1	2	3	4	5
Not at all for this reason		Somewhat		Very much for this reason

1. ____**I don't know why.** I don't really have any goals for the class, and I don't expect to do very well.

2. ____**Because I have to.** Circumstances necessitate it. In order to get good grades, impress teachers, friends, or parents, or keep my scholarship, I must do well in this class.

3. ____**Because I should.** I'd feel guilty if I didn't do well, and would worry that I was wasting myself or my abilities. Rather than feeling compelled by circumstances to try to do well, I compel myself.

4. ____**Because I want to.** I fully agree with the value of this class, and do not have to force myself to try to do well. Even at times when the material or assignment is not very interesting, I have no trouble keeping going because I believe in what I am doing.

5. ____**Because I enjoy it.** I am interested and engaged while trying to do well. I feel a sense of competence and mastery while doing it, and the sense that I am expanding my understanding of topics that deeply interest me.

25 ENGAGEMENT
CIVIC ENGAGEMENT
Constance Flanagan and Brian D. Christens

This op-ed activity is an opportunity for students to take a stand on and communicate their opinions on a civic/community issue, to acknowledge other perspectives, and to draw from research in support of their stand.

CONCEPT

Civic engagement refers to the actions that citizens take to create the kind of community and society they want to live in. Civic engagement does not mean that people give up their self-interest but that they come to see their interests in relation to fellow citizens and to the common good. As Rousseau (1762/2008) explained in his treatise on the social contract, "the undertakings which bind us to the social body are obligatory only because they are mutual; and their nature is such that in fulfilling them we cannot work for others without working for ourselves" (p. 36). When they became engaged in civic issues, citizens clarify their own positions and come to appreciate the different perspectives of fellow citizens. Through civil discourse and collective action, individuals realize that they are members of the public, who constitute the sovereign authority in a democracy.

MATERIALS
NEEDED

Students bring to class examples of op-eds from newspapers (hard copy or online) or opinion pieces from online media or blogs.

INSTRUCTIONS

Pioneered by the *New York Times* in 1970, the op-ed (which stands for "opposite to the editorial page" and not for "opinion editorial," as is often thought) is now a common genre of newspaper article. It is written by a person who is not a member of the newspaper's editorial board, including people who are not professional journalists. The style and format of an op-ed are similar to an editorial piece; it explicitly stakes out and defends an opinion on a public issue. Individuals, and not editorial boards, write them, so op-eds are often highly personal. An early editor of the op-ed page at the *New York Times* described the makings of a good op-ed to a contributing writer: "The most successful pieces have been highly individualistic, opinionated and pungent. . . . You will not get arrested if the piece is also witty" (Shafer, 2010).

The op-ed activity can be used in a variety of courses that emphasize civic engagement and university–community interactions or those that involve discussions of civic/community issues and social change. The activity may prove particularly useful

DOI: 10.1037/14042-026
Activities for Teaching Positive Psychology: A Guide for Instructors, J. J. Froh and A. C. Parks (Editors)

in courses that involve a service–learning component and those that engage students in community-based research. The activity takes place in three stages and in different class meetings.

Stage 1

Students bring to class examples of op-eds that they have found from local, student, and national newspapers or online blogs. In small (three- to four-member) groups, students discuss what they consider to be the elements of a good op-ed, and the class then summarizes those elements. Along with input from the instructor, these elements become the bases for class members' work on writing their own op-eds. Based on doing this activity in multiple classes, we provide a handout in Appendix 25.1 on "Getting Started on Writing Your First Op-Ed" and "Elements of a Good Op-Ed."

In preparation for the second phase (peer reviews), the class also discusses the peer-review process. The goal of the peer review is to practice civil discourse—to disagree on points of view and perspectives but to do so with respect for the rights of one another. The peer-review process is meant to help fellow members of the class to clarify their points of view, to appreciate alternative perspectives, and to communicate clearly where they stand.

Stage 2

Each student writes his or her first op-ed draft (aiming for a piece of 300–500 words) and brings four hard copies to class. Note that this is somewhat shorter than op-eds in many newspapers, but it enables time for peer reviews and encourages students to be concise. (See Appendix 25.1 for tips on getting started and for elements of a good op-ed.) Students share their op-ed drafts and engage in civil and constructive peer reviews of one another's work. Ideally, this takes place in groups of three to four students (who constitute a public) so that all members of the group share their opinions on the issue and provide each writer civil and constructive feedback for ways to clarify his or her argument.

Stage 3

The first two stages are in-class activities. The third stage involves students revising their op-eds on the basis of the feedback from the peer reviews, and turning in both the originals and revised drafts to the instructor. Students should be encouraged to seek outlets for publishing their op-eds—most newspapers have a system for electronic submissions of op-eds.

DISCUSSION   The op-ed activity is a short writing assignment, but one that is thought provoking and interactive. Indeed, it is often more difficult to condense an argument into a succinct and pithy paper than to expound on it at length. Moreover, the impact of the assignment extends beyond the substantive material and the classroom setting. It engages students—in cognitive and emotional ways—with their classmates as fellow citizens.

Feedback and reflections from students who have completed the assignment confirm that this activity can have such impacts. One student wrote,

> The op-ed exercise forces students to imagine a "public"—whether fellow students on campus, local community members, city officials, or fellow Americans—and to craft an argument concerning some "common good" issue that engages those members of the public as fellow citizens or stakeholders.

In addition, the activity involves students in a process of reflection and research on their opinions on social issues. In doing so, it promotes the habit of identifying evidence in support of an argument. As one student wrote,

> This assignment certainly helped me to clarify my views on the issue I chose to write about. Previous to this assignment, it would have been easy for me to let my emotions get the best and simply write on more of a whim. Due to the nature of this assignment, I was forced to step back, analyze my perspective, and find supporting evidence.

Students often come across arguments from different positions on their civic/community issue while seeking evidence to support their positions. Some of these counterarguments include evidence in support of other positions. As a result, some students modify their initial positions. Others, like the student who wrote the following reflection, strengthen their views through this process:

> This process helped me clarify my stand on the issue because the research required exposed me to other points of view. As I read these other points of view, I was mentally making counterarguments, which strengthened my stand on the issue.

The clarity that is achieved in the research process is reinforced in the peer-review phase of the activity as students present their arguments to one another and receive feedback. In the words of one student,

> After writing down my thoughts about women's shelters and then also talking them out during the peer-review process, I feel much more comfortable speaking publicly about my opinion. I think the process really allowed me to bring my thoughts and ideas on the issue to a concise group of ideas in my mind, whereas before it was a little more vague.

Students also report that the peer-review process involved diverse opinions and was effective in identifying where common ground might be found on their civic/community issue.

Finally, many students report that their experiences of this activity encourage them to become more actively engaged in civic and community issues. Through completing this activity, they gain confidence in their opinions and their ability to communicate them. They have an experience of attempting to convince others of the merit of their views in a supportive and civil environment. This leads them to not only a greater understanding of civic and community issues but also a heightened sense of the possibility that they can make a difference on these issues. "[The op-ed activity] not only helped make me be a better student but also a better, more informed citizen."[1]

---

[1]To better grasp this topic, instructors and students are encouraged to consult the following sources: Arendt (1958); Dewey (1927); and Elshtain (1995).

REFERENCES

Arendt, H. (1958). The public realm. In *The human condition* (pp. 50–58). Chicago, IL: University of Chicago Press.

Dewey, J. (1927). *The public and its problems.* New York, NY: Holt.

Elshtain, J. B. (1995). *Democracy on trial.* New York, NY: Basic Books.

Rousseau, J.-J. (2008). *The social contract.* New York, NY: Cosimo. (Original work published 1762)

Shafer, J. (2010, September 27). The op-ed's back pages: A press scholar explains how the *New York Times* op-ed page got started. *Slate.* Retrieved from http://www.slate.com/id/2268829/

Appendix 25.1

GETTING STARTED ON WRITING YOUR FIRST OP-ED

A. Consider an issue that you care about deeply—one on which you have an opinion.

- Write a few short statements of your opinions—so you are clear on where you stand on the issue.
- Write a few short statements of opposing points of view on the issue—to remind yourself of other perspectives.

B. Imagine the audience to whom you are speaking (e.g., fellow students, fellow citizens in your community or nation, policymakers, philanthropists).

- What do they need to know?
- What are compelling arguments that they will hear from you?
- What information will help them see your point of view?
- What appeals will be most persuasive (e.g., case study, statistics, dollars saved, appeal to personal values or social roles)?

ELEMENTS OF A GOOD OP-ED

- Develop a short, catchy title that captures essence of your message.
- Decide on your main point—what you want readers to take away.
- Establish the urgency or importance of the issue in the first paragraph.
- Provide a context for your argument.
- Take a stand on the issue and make your stand relevant to a wider audience.
- Use words that the general public would understand (avoid jargon and terms that only others in your discipline or classes would understand).
- Use short declarative statements and pointed questions.
- Be passionate, but step back from the issue or event and get perspective—develop a reasoned argument. An op-ed is not a harangue.
- Use evidence (e.g., data, studies, cost–benefit argument) to support your position. (You can state this succinctly and refer readers to websites, and other sources for more details.)
- Acknowledge opposing viewpoints, but be prepared to challenge them.
- Do not use personal attacks or uncivil language.
- Conclude with a call to action or vision (i.e., what readers can do or why fellow citizens should share your vision).

INDEX

ABOUT THE EDITORS

Jeffrey J. Froh, PsyD, is an associate professor of psychology at Hofstra University and a leading scholar in positive youth psychology. His research, which has been featured in mainstream media such as *The Wall Street Journal* and *The Washington Post*, focuses on the wellsprings, assessment, outcomes, and enhancement of gratitude in children and adolescents. He is past associate editor for the *Journal of Positive Psychology*, and his research has been funded by the John Templeton Foundation.

Acacia C. Parks, PhD, is an assistant professor of psychology at Hiram College. She received her PhD from the University of Pennsylvania, where she worked under Martin Seligman at the Positive Psychology Center. Her research focuses on the efficacy of positive interventions and the psychological and behavioral characteristics of individuals who use them. She serves as an associate editor of the *Journal of Positive Psychology* and was recently guest editor of the special issue "Positive Psychology in Higher Education." She is also editor of a forthcoming handbook of positive psychological interventions from Wiley-Blackwell. Dr. Parks is an active teacher of positive psychology and critical writing, and maintains a blog at *Psychology Today*.